Successful Single Adult Ministry:

It Can Happen in Your Church

Krista Swan Welsh, Editor

 STANDARD PUBLISHING
Cincinnati, Ohio   3219

Library of Congress Cataloging-in-Publication Data

Successful single adult ministry.

    Bibliography: p.
    Includes index.
    1. Church work with single people. I. Welsh,
      Krista Swan
BV4437.S83   1987   259   87-10048
ISBN 0-87403-229-6

Sculpture on cover by Jan Wimmer, Cincinnati, Ohio

Dedication

This book is dedicated to the 1983-85 "Fellowship" class, of the Clovernook Christian Church, Cincinnati, Ohio, and to its fearless leaders, Jim and Phyllis Grogg. "Fellowship," you were typical Christian single adults, which means you were nothing less than terrific. May this book recall a lot of fond memories.

Contents

A Brief Introduction

It was 1985 when I first approached Marge Miller, then Director of New Products at Standard Publishing, with an idea for a singles book. After all, I had been living on my own for two years by then, and I had a slew of single anecdotes I was sure the world was dying to hear. I was ready to write a book that would amuse and inspire my readers.

Marge had other ideas. "Why not write a more practical book, that would help ministers with single adult ministries in their churches?"

Well, it wasn't what I had in mind, and I certainly did not feel *that* knowledgeable on single adulthood. But I had a few contacts with people who did know about singles and the local church, so I enlisted their expertise and together we wrote *Successful Single Adult Ministry: It Can Happen In Your Church*. I have to admit, what these writers have to share with you is better than my single anecdotes. Not always as amusing, but definitely more useable.

It may appear that the different authors hold different views about single adult ministry. For example, one author may recommend calling a married couple to lead your single adult group, while another writer advocates letting the single adults lead themselves. However, I believe all the authors agree on a couple of important things: 1) every single adult group is unique, and it may take a couple of tries at things before you hit upon a program tailored for your singles; 2) the theme of our writings echoes the words of Terry Fisher, which can be found on pages 42 and 43 of this book:

> Success is not determined by numbers or type of program. An effective singles ministry is one that meets the needs of singles and spurs them on to spiritual and emotional maturity.

Happy reading! May this book be a source of guidance as you commit yourself to the task of building up single adults to finding a closer walk with our Lord, and a place of service in His church. And if this book truly does help make a successful single adult ministry happen in *your* church, then to God be the glory.

Krista Swan Welsh, Editor

CHAPTER ONE

About This Chapter's Author

Dennis Chamberlain is currently working as pastor in charge of Single Adult Ministries and Counseling Services at Crossroads Christian Church in Corona, California. He has been trained as a minister (B.A., San Jose Bible College) and counselor (M.A., University of Santa Clara).

Dennis is a single adult, and has been since the death of his wife in 1980. In addition to his work at Crossroads, he also serves as consultant, resource person, and retreat speaker for various church groups. Dennis has been specializing in single adult work since 1976.

Contact information: Crossroads Christian Church
P.O. Box 1775
Corona, CA 91720
(714) 371-2741

–1–

Let's Start at the Beginning ... Who Are Single Adults?

by Dennis Chamberlain

The year was 1980. Christmas, no longer "just around the corner," rose up everywhere in a swelling tide of music, laughter, and traditional festivities. As usual, my wife and I had moved into the holiday season with the same excitement and intensity of a couple of five-year-olds. And, although this was always a very busy time of the year for us, we were determined to enjoy ourselves completely.

It had been a very demanding year with long hours at the office, unfinished projects with unreasonable deadlines, and never quite enough time for a couple to enjoy each other's company. There was no reason to believe that 1980 would be any different than the other nine Christmases we had shared together.

However, as is often the case with those who encounter personal tragedy, I didn't know quite what to do when I learned that my wife was dying. As we drove to the hospital, I was aware that my wife was experiencing a great deal of physical distress; both of us were more afraid than we wanted to admit. As we talked in her room at the hospital, we knew that something was seriously wrong ... but we didn't know how to put it into words.

Finally, my wife put her hand on mine and looked intently at me. She said, "I think this might be the time ... what should we do?" I knew what she meant—but I didn't know what to do! I told her that we would have to

11

trust God and face whatever came with courage and hope. These were brave words to speak, but I did not feel very brave as I walked from her room on the morning of her death. I simply felt numb, confused, and very much alone.

Single Adults in America

I soon learned that as a newly widowed person I had joined the ranks of literally millions of other individuals who were "alone and on their own," for it was in that same year of 1980 that the United States government compiled its exhaustive national head-count called the Census. The figures compiled in this massive data bank made it very clear that "single adults" formed a large and growing segment of the American adult population (almost 40% nationally). And many of these singles (some never-married, some "single again" as a result of death or divorce) were, like myself, in need of guidance and community support from fellow Christians. But— where could one find such help?

Fortunately, I belonged to a congregation which (though small in size) had an active outreach program for single people. I was able to meet others who could identify with my needs and questions; and I didn't feel like an oddball because I was an unmarried adult. The unfortunate part of the picture was that this was not typical of our churches across the country. In fact, the dramatic growth of the single adult sector (particularly the "single again" category) during the last decade had led to a very serious problem: there were literally millions of these "singles" walking around, and proportionally very few church ministries designed to assist them. Many churches were equipped with active adult ministries, but they were typically geared for married adults and, perhaps, college-age adults.

Today's single adult has become the subject of much study and discussion—not only within the church but outside as well. Thinkers and policy-shapers in our society today have noted that among the significant changes and developments within our society (especially in the last decade), few stand out as prominently as the "single adult phenomenon."

John Naisbitt, cultural analyst and social forecaster, offers a fascinating and somewhat sobering account of the gradual transformation of American society—especially as these changes have affected family life. According to Naisbitt, although most of today's adults were raised in a typical nuclear family ... as of 1980, there is no longer any such thing as a "typical family." In fact, the typical or traditional family model (never-divorced husband and wife; two children; husband works/wife a homemaker) claims only a miniscule seven percent of today's population.

Naisbitt argues that the basic building block of society today is shifting from the family to the individual:

> More than ever before people live alone—a remarkable one in four is a single-person household, compared with one in ten in 1955. These individuals are the young who have not yet married, the elderly, the newly divorced. And they are so numerous that the basic building block of society is now the individual, rather than the family ... These new family models will be with us for a long time, and American families will grow even more diverse.[1]

The concept of society which is primarily "individual" in its orientation is unsettling to most of us—even to those of us who are single. Nevertheless, we must face certain facts about this development in our society.

The Never-Marrieds

The single adult sector referred to as "never-marrieds" will most likely continue to expand. Many of

---

[1]Naisbitt, John. *Megatrends: Ten New Directions Transforming Our Lives,* Warner Books, 1982, pages 232, 233.

these people today are deferring marriage until their late twenties and thirties—for a variety of reasons. For some, it is a decision based upon economic considerations ("I'll live at home until I finish college and get a job"); others are discovering that to be unmarried will be viewed as an asset by many employers today who place a high value upon an employee's availability and mobility. The single person can travel the globe on a moment's notice without putting a strain on family members, and they will most likely be available for this at a lower cost than a family man would be.

Many single people are also choosing co-habitation— if not "instead of" marriage, at least as a transition into marriage. Also, the availability of young, marriageable women is not what it used to be. Today, more than ever before, young, unmarried women are thinking in terms of "careers" during their twenties rather than marriage. They still value marriage and family, but it will be postponed until certain vocational and financial goals can be accomplished. One last factor which is having a very significant impact upon the minds of the never-married group has to do with a certain anxiety concerning marriage, specifically related to marriage failure.

Because of today's high divorce rates, as well as the constant media attention directed at the commoness of marital unhappiness, many single people have become literally afraid of marriage. As one young woman put it, "I don't want to go through the horrible experience of divorce . . . I went through it with my parents, and I know a lot of people who have gotten divorced. I'm going to wait until I'm sure." And wait she will; for according to current statistical data, the proportion of single men and women between the ages of 25 and 35 has almost doubled since 1970. Today the median age for first marriages among women is at the highest point ever recorded in American history (Men: 25.4 years; Women: 23 years).[2]

[2]*Marital Status and Living Arrangements: March 1984;* Current Population Reports; Population Characteristics, Series P-20, no. 399; U.S. Dept. of Commerce, Bureau of the Census; issued 1985.

The never-married group clearly has the lion's share of overall territory within the general territory of single adults (37 million or 54%), and the majority of these (65%) fall between the ages of 18 and 30.[3] From the standpoint of these various factors, it appears likely that the never-married population will continue to be a significant ingredient in the make-up of our society.

The Elderly

Since the turn of the century, no other population group (age group) has developed as dramatically as the elderly (65 years and older). In the year 1880, this group accounted for about 3% of the entire adult population; according to the 1980 census data, they now represent 11% and this growth will continue. This development is largely the result of lower fertility rates, increased longevity, and an aging "baby boom" generation.

Sometimes referred to as "the greying of America," this trend significantly affects the overall single adult picture. At any given period of history a large percentage of elderly grouping is made up of those who are widowed; in fact, in 1985 those aged 65 years and above numbered almost 27 million—10 million of whom were widowed with another 2½ million "alone and on their own" for various other reasons (never-married, divorced, convalescent home placements). The U.S. Bureau of the Census projects that this population segment will expand for at least another 50 years. Based upon these projections, a recently published report on population trends and demographics declares that, "between (the years) 2010 and 2020 a revolutionary change in age composition is scheduled to set in, with the proportion of elderly rising swiftly from 13-14% to 21-22%."[4] The implications from this trend for the local

[3] *Marital Status and Living Arrangement: March 1985;* forthcoming current Population Reports; Series P-20, no. 410; issued July 1986.

[4] *The Population of the United States; Historical Trends and Future Projections,* by Donald J. Bogue, Free Press, 1985, p. 61.

15

congregation are manifold; however, it is clear that an ever-widening stream of older, single people will flow into the church from this segment of the population.

The Divorced

As disheartening as it may be, divorce is now a firmly entrenched part of our societal structure. There are several ways to analyze this development: we can note that in the year 1910 approximately 948,000 marriages were recorded for the entire country and about 83,000 divorces were granted. When we examine the current figures (1985), we learn that 2.4 million marriages were recorded and 1.2 million divorces were granted! This reflects a marriage/divorce ratio of roughly ten to one (in 1910) versus today's ratio of ten to five.

A second method for analyzing the divorce phenomena is called the "Lifetable Analysis." In this method projections are made based upon census data and certain hypothetical assumptions. According to the Department of Health and Human services, a Lifetable Analysis based upon a 1980 population sample shows that approximately 43% of the marriages begun in 1980 will end in divorce.[5] Another approach, widely used for marriage and divorce research, is the "divorce rate" method. The divorce rate indicates the number of men and women per one thousand (married population) who get divorced each year.[6] Current rates are at about 22/1000 which means that each year about 2% of all married couples get divorced (approximately 1.2 million

[5]Phone interview with Barbara Wilson of the Department of Health and Human Services, Branch of Marriage and Family Statistics, October 24, 1986.

[6]The rate may be used to indicate general population features or special categories; i.e., the divorce rate within the general population is currently 5/1000; although this rate is widely used in newspaper reports, it does not offer an accurate enough picture. The rates quoted in this chapter are based upon the married population, women, age 15 years and above.

couples in 1985).[7] Very much like a "mortality rate," this measurement shows how many marriages are "dying off" each year within the overall married population.

From this data we can easily see that divorce has not only become a well-established practice in our society, but it has also steadily increased with each passing decade. For example, in the year 1940 the divorced sector made up only 1.4% of the adult population, whereas in 1985 this same group comprised 7.7% of all adults.

From a ministry point of view this translates into over 13 million "walking wounded" single people who are in serious need of the good news of Jesus Christ and the healing care of the church. Will the divorce trend continue? It is my opinion that it will, although perhaps at a slower pace. For this trend to reverse, or even level off, it will require an extensive values-shift on the part of our society, particularly in regard to those values pertaining to relationship commitment, sacrificial love, and the postponement of self-gratification.

Identifying Single Adults and Their Needs

Certainly the most common designation assigned the non-married person today is the word "single." Although this term is useful for the sake of general, organizational purposes, it should not be assumed that all single people like it. For some, it can be a bit offensive since it identifies a person strictly in terms of marital status (not to mention that the word "single" brings to mind the images of one-dollar bills, small motel beds, or just one scoop of ice cream), and marital status *is* a sensitive issue for many single people.

Whether we like it or not, it does seem that we are stuck with the label; however, sensitive church leaders will minimize their usage of it and attempt to emphasize

[7]National Center for Health Statistics; Advance report of Final Divorce Statistics, 1984, *Monthly Vital Statistics Report,* Vol. 35, no. 6, Supp. DHHS Pub. no. (PHS) 86-1120; Public Health Service, Hyattsville, MD., Sept. 25, 1986.

the more central fact that singles are *persons* and *adults* who happen to be single. Also when the label has to be used, a good compromise is the term "single adults." This may seem to be a very minor point, but I have found that a little sensitivity can go a long way.

When we speak of single adults and the singles ministry, we are not referring to a monolithic group. There are four basic sub-groups that can be identified beneath the umbrella term "single": 1) the never-marrieds; 2) the widowed; 3) the divorced; and 4) the separated.
The breakdown for each sub-group can be seen in the following diagram:

Total Single Adult Population (18 years and over)
By Marital Status

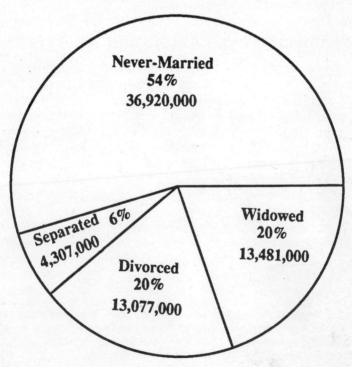

According to the 1985 census data, these four subgroups represent a total of 67.8 million people, which is approximately 40% of the overall adult population.[8]

Total Population By Marital Status (18 years and over)

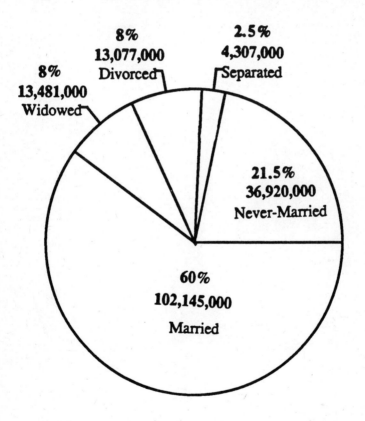

[8]The 40% figure reflects the singles population on the national level; those living in rural areas will see a much smaller ratio, according to Arlene Salater of the Bureau of Census (approximately 28%), while those in metropolitan areas will see a higher ratio (New York 48%; Houston 36%; Los Angeles 46%).

If we examine the various age distributions, we discover that the vast majority of never-marrieds are between the ages of 18 and 30; most of the divorced and separated are between 30 and 54 years of age; and the bulk of widowed people fall into the 55-and-up age bracket.

Total Single Adult Population By Age
(18 years and over, "Separated" not included)

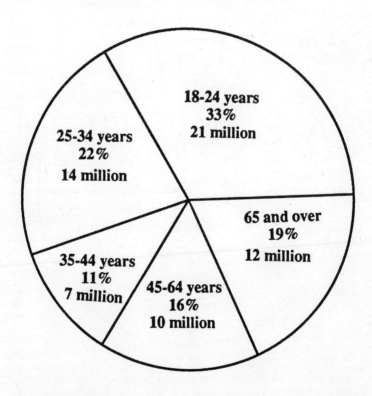

Information on pie graphs from *Marital Status and Living Arrangements: March 1985;* forthcoming current Population Reports; Series P-20, No. 410; issued July 1986.

Understanding these distinctions is a necessary step toward understanding what a single adult ministry is and how it should function. Obviously, the particular needs and interests will vary significantly from group to group; for example, a 23-year-old collegiate will not be very interested in talking about the bereavement process with a widower, nor will a 30-year-old never-married person get very excited about divorce recovery issues. This is not to say that these various types of single people have nothing at all in common ... it's just that the differences are very significant, and if they aren't taken seriously, the result (programatically) can be disastrous. As if this were not complicated enough, there are even more distinctions which deserve the careful consideration of those who plan and coordinate a single adult ministry. We must ask, "are we dealing with single parents?"; and, "are they the parents of teenagers or toddlers?"; or, "are we dealing with young, never-marrieds in college, or are they working full-time?"

When these kinds of distinctions are understood, and even more importantly the needs and interests they represent, then an intelligent strategy can be designed for an effective ministry to these people. However, the emphasis must be upon meeting the *actual needs* of single people and not upon the needs which married folks and church officials *think* are most important. This can easily become a point for misunderstanding between church leaders and single people. Stereotypes and myths abound when it comes to the single adult sector. For example:

- All singles are "swingers" who spend every free moment looking for a party.
- Singles are irresponsible and undependable.
- Singles are oversexed and generally promiscuous.
- All singles are looking for a partner to marry.
- The problems of singles will be solved by marriage.
- Single parents don't provide a good home life for their children.
- Singles aren't married because they are basically selfish and/or immature.

21

Stereotypes like these hinder an effective outreach ministry. None of the above statements is completely true or even mostly true! Yet, these same mythical ideas are in the minds (if not on the lips) of many a church leader. At leadership conferences and training seminars, I have often heard such comments as: "If we begin a singles ministry, won't it just turn into a dating club?" Or, "if singles come into our church in force, how can we counteract the worldly spirit they will bring?"

If we are to develop an intelligent response to single adults and their needs, we must look below the surface of these common generalizations as follows: 1) Single adults are not necessarily "swingers" because they enjoy a high degree of social activity. It is true that many single people have more free time and disposable income than married couples ... but many don't (for example: single parents, students, and many young career people). Many single people detest the nightclub scene and the party pattern.

2) Single adults who have not learned the disciplines of marriage and family and who have become accustomed to large amounts of freedom and independence can certainly take on the appearance, if not the reality, of an irresponsible life-style. Then again, some of the best and most loyal church workers have always been single adults who have used this freedom and mobility for the Kingdom of God.

3) Most single adults will agree that sexuality is a very important issue to them. In general, it seems that previously married singles find it to be more troublesome and pressing than do the never-marrieds.[9] It is also true that sexual promiscuity exists in the single adult sector; however, this is clearly not applicable to *all* single people! Many single people work hard at maintaining disciplined life-styles and will likely feel insulted if they are stereotyped in this way. In addition to this, most of these people are aware of the well-publicized fact that promis-

[9]*Singles, Myths and Realities* by Leonard Cargan and Matthew Melko, Sage Publications, Inc., 1982, Chapter 7.

cuity is also a serious problem for married people. In light of these considerations, it is clear that a supportive and encouraging approach, mixed with a degree of humility, is the best way to respond to the "sexual promiscuity" issue.

4) Generally speaking, the only marriages that will be threatened by single people are the same marriages that will also be threatened by other married people as well. These marriages are susceptible to danger for a variety of reasons, and it simply confuses the real issue to project the blame onto singles. Most single people that I have met are interested in meeting other singles, not someone else's spouse.

5) Although most single people will marry (or remarry), it is not accurate to label all singles as "marriage hungry." As noted earlier in this chapter, more single people than ever before are deferring marriage rather than rushing into it. But, perhaps more important than this is that the topic of marriage is a sensitive point to many single adults today. They do not appreciate the jokes, facetious remarks, and innuendos about marriage that married people often direct their way. Single people prefer to be regarded as individuals who are pursuing their own multi-faceted life goals like anyone else—not as a type of "half-person" maintaining a kind of holding pattern on life until they can get married.

6) Though it is true that single-parent families often face high levels of stress and turmoil and perhaps more transition difficulties than two-parent families, many of these single parents do an excellent job in regard to child rearing and parent/child relationship development. This may be due to the fact that they are forced to try harder because of the absence of a partner. Additionally, if divorce has taken place, there is often less conflict in the home than there was before the divorce.

The area that does seem to suffer is that of family discipline. Single parents are often single mothers[10]

---

[10]Women comprise approximately 90% of all custodial parents; *U.S. News and World Report* interview with Professor Lenore Weitzman of Stanford University; June 1985, p. 63.

who are trying to do everything under the sun that a typical, two-parent family would do. They very easily become fatigued; they may become too permissive (or too strict) because of guilt; or they may just not have the time to keep up with their kids and do everything else also. Whatever the case may be, they *can* provide very good homes, and they need all the help and encouragement they can get.

What a Minister Needs to Know About Today's Single Adult

Getting beyond these myths and stereotypes is an important beginning step for the church leader who plans to minister to single people. The next step is to develop an accurate picture of the various needs and interests of single adults. While it is true that single adults have the same basic needs as all other adults, it is also true that single adults represent what could be called a "special interest group." It is to these special needs or interests that the wise minister will direct his attention. Because if they are ignored or misunderstood the result will be irrelevance and ineffectiveness in an area that is "white unto harvest."

Single people today are looking to the church to satisfy three basic needs: 1) The need to be understood and acknowledged within the general church community; 2) The need to be treated as equal citizens (alongside those who are married) in the Kingdom of God; and 3) The need for a healthy social environment within the church.

The first two needs relate to the fact that most churches are decidedly "nuclear family" in their overall orientation. Because of this, the typical single person doesn't fit in. As one single man expressed it, "I attend church occasionally, but that is about as far as it goes. My church is geared for the couples and families, and because I am single I don't really fit in very well. I don't think they understand about being single ... or if they do they never talk about it." It means a great deal to a single adult when the preacher includes the non-married group in his greetings from the pulpit, in his sermon illustrations, and in other common, public references. When I address a group of adults in a church meeting, I will often say something like, "Whether you are married or single, whether you have a family or you are alone—today's lesson can apply to your life." This is a simple technique to adopt, and it communicates to the single person the idea that "your church knows you and acknowledges your uniqueness within the body."

Closely related to this is the problem of "perceived inequality" of many single adults. This occurs when a church has a marriage and family emphasis that has gotten out of balance. More specifically, it means that the nuclear family concept has become the chief ingredient in the overall identity of the congregation, and, as a result, those who don't fall into this category are viewed as second-best. In this type of church, the married couples tend to view singles as unfulfilled, incomplete, human beings, with their lives in a "holding pattern" until marriage occurs. This viewpoint reflects much ignorance, if not a touch of arrogance as well. The truth is that genuine wholeness and fulfillment is just as possible for the single person as for the married; and, indeed, we have some very outstanding models of fulfilled, dynamic single adults in the Bible (for example— Ezekiel, Naomi, Daniel, John the Baptist, Jesus, and Paul).

Church leaders would also do well to re-evaluate the nuclear family model in light of the Bible. It appears that an "extended family" model (husband and wife, parents, servants, children) more accurately expresses the Biblical norm, whereas the nuclear model seems to be a development that has arisen for the most part from the industrial revolution and the modernization of the western world.[11]

[11]The thesis that the nuclear family model developed from industrialization and modernization in the West is strongly challenged today. Cf. E.A. Wrigley, *Population and History,* New York: McGraw-Hill, 1969; *Montaillou,* New York: Vintage, 1979 by Emmanuel Ladurie; and especially *The War Over The Family: Capturing the Middle Ground* by Berger and Berger; Anchor Press, Doubleday; 1984; pg. 85-104.

This is not to say that the extended family model is superior just because it is Biblical, but rather to point out that today's common bias on the part of many Christians in favor of the nuclear model as the "proper Christian way" is simply a bias without any basis in the Bible. Why not develop a family model that allows all individuals (including singles) a family identity within the church?

The need for a healthy social environment within the church is something that is felt very keenly by today's single. It is also something that is commonly ignored and misunderstood by many church leaders. Single adults, like adults in general, enjoy and need a certain amount of social interaction. However, unlike those who are married, they often have no basic home unit to meet those needs. Loneliness is a central factor in the lives of most single people (whether they admit it or not), and when they cannot meet their social needs in the home or in the church they often turn to the nightclub scene or some other secular source. It appears that many church leaders are reluctant to address this problem. They will develop social activities for children and youth, married couples, and senior citizens ... but little or nothing for the single person—especially those beyond college age. Sometimes this reluctance is based upon a fear that "things might get out of hand" or "we may start up a dating-mill." Regardless of what the source is for this posture, the facts will not change: single people have social needs, and they will look to the church for assistance. If the church turns them away, they will go elsewhere.

For the minister working with a small congregation, this may come as a distressing thought; after all, doesn't it require the people and means of a large congregation to develop such a social program? This may seem to be the case on the surface of things, but it is certainly not true. The small congregation (under 200 members), if it so chooses, is capable of helping single adults meet their social needs (at least partially).

There are essentially three ways a small congregation can meet the social needs of its single adults: 1) by providing part-time staff oversight for your single people; this could be done by a Christian education or youth minister. In my first position as an associate minister, I was allowed to spend 10-15 hours each week in developing a singles program. Our congregation was small (100-125 members), but within the first year we had a core group of 15-25 single adults; and within three years we were seeing 50-60 regulars each week. We were able to provide an active and wholesome social program which caught the attention of the larger churches in the area. It can be done!

2) By intra-church networking: this method works by organizing singles from various churches in a way that allows them to meet other singles and socialize, while at the same time keep their roots in their home church. This can be done by staff, elders, or selected leaders from your group of single people.

3) By encouraging your single people to explore other singles' programs, at least for the social benefits. Most singles ministries that I have examined have no interest in proselytizing people from other churches; in fact, large single adult programs are almost always made up of people from many church backgrounds and locations. They are not so concerned with what church one belongs to or doctrinal differences—they desire simple fellowship and enjoyable social activities with others of like faith. An important point here is that a minister or elder must "give permission" by way of encouragement and support. If this is done properly, your single people will discover sources for social involvement outside of their church, while at the same time remain loyal to their home church.

Once a congregation begins to develop a warm and accepting environment for single people, not only will they begin to show up in your church ... they will also begin to talk openly about their particular "issues." What are these issues? The issues are important to know, from a program perspective, because this knowledge will enable you to "reach these people where they really live." There are seven categories of concern that most single people share in common:

1. Interpersonal Relationships
2. Personal Growth
3. Life-style Challenges
4. Mystique of Marriage
5. Crisis Recovery
6. Parenting Concerns
7. Spiritual Life Development

Single people are concerned about how to develop meaningful relationships with the opposite sex ... whether this be in dating situations or in simple friendships. This is basically a very normal and healthy concern and one that echoes the concern of God Almighty at the time of creation ("It is not good for man to be alone ... I will provide a woman for him"—Genesis 2:18, my paraphrase). The problem is that there is much confusion "out there" in the world of relationships and much challenge as well. Because of this, single people are interested in learning all they can on the subject. As church leaders, we need to ask the question, "Is my congregation a place where single people can find guidance, support, and sensitivity as they attempt to learn about dating, relating, and mating?"

The term "personal growth," although much overused, points to a very high-interest area of single adult life. Generally, this term refers to personal development revolving around such issues as self-esteem, identity crisis, mental health, maturation, self-awareness, and personality conflicts. It has been said that we live today in a "psychological age"—and so we do. Whether for the good or the bad, many single people are strongly focused on developmental aspects of their lives. And what better place for them to explore these complex issues than the church?

Life-style challenges mean, "With what do I, as a single person in modern America, struggle as I conduct my everday life?" The answer to this is far more complex than most church leaders and married couples would ever guess. And it can be answered differently by different "types" of singles. For example, the never-married, career-type single adult often has a high percentage of disposable income, plus comparatively few financial responsibilities, plus much free time, plus very little accountability to anyone ... do you begin to see the problem? (Perhaps you're thinking, I would like to be afflicted with this problem!) The truth is, this peculiar setup presents a great challenge for the concerned single person. It is truly a two-sided coin: on one side there are the almost limitless possibilities for enjoying "the good life," while on the other side an incredibly strong current pulling one toward self-indulgence and hedonism.

Another example would be the middle-aged, divorced man who must struggle with sexual abstinence. He was previously accustomed to regular sexual relations with a woman, and now he is socializing with Christian women and asking himself, "How do I function like someone who doesn't relate sexually to a woman?" Or consider the successful career woman in her early thirties who is dynamic, independent, and financially secure. She has begun to realize that success and independence can be a blessing and a curse. These are only a few of the contemporary life-style challenges in which single people are enmeshed.

Harold Ivan Smith, popular author and conference speaker, has coined the phrase "mystique of marriage" to identify a major stress point among single adults. He notes that it is very common for singles to put off or suspend significant decisions until marriage and that many singles do *feel* (not necessarily *believe)* that once they get married "everything will be good." Whether singles admit it or not (and they are less likely to admit it around married couples who are fond of saying, "when are you going to get married?"), they do think a lot about marriage. They are concerned and they would like to learn as much as possible on the subject. Because singles have a different perspective than most married couples, a good approach is to create a setting where the church can ask its single people, "What do you want to talk about in regard to the topic of marriage?"

Most of the interest in crisis recovery comes from

singles who are divorced or widowed. This can be a life-change that leaves a person feeling "dashed and broken in the street of life," or as though catapulted into an entirely new universe. These kinds of marital crises go far beyond the loss of a loved one and the death of a relationship; there may also be family disruption, re-entry into the workplace, learning how to be a single person, working through an identity crisis, and more! There are thirteen-plus million adults today who are looking for help in these areas.

Single parenting is another world unto itself. These are the singles who have comparatively little disposable income, little free time, and often little energy left at the end of the day. Lyle Schaller refers to them as "the young ex-homemakers" and describes the increase of this group as "... one of the most radical, but largely ignored changes in the population that has taken place during the past two decades."[12]

According to recent census data,[13] about 14 million children are presently living with just one parent (an increase of six million since 1970), and the vast major-ity of these parents are divorced or separated women. Based upon current figures, it is estimated that over half of all children in the United States today will at some time in their growing-up years live with only one par-ent.[14] Each year over a million children enter this sector of the population, entering into the pain and stress this situation brings as well.

Single parents bring a number of serious concerns to the church. Beyond the crisis recovery issues related to death or divorce, there are economic hardships to face, behavioral problems with the children as a reaction to the change, the adjustment to a one-parent system of family government, re-entry into the workplace and the continual problem of loneliness and burn-out. Stanford

[12]"The Parish Paper," Yokefellow Institute, Oct. 1979, Vol. 9, no. 4.

[13]*ibid.,* Current Population Reports, Series P-20, no. 399, pages 1-6.

[14]*U.S. News and World Report,* April 12, 1982, p. 62.

Professor Lenore Weitzman, author of *The Divorce Revolution,* states that on the average divorced women and minor children experience a 73% drop in their standard of living in the first year after divorce (men, in contrast, experience a 42% increase).[15] She goes on to say that 90% of all custodial parents are women.

Willard Black, Director of the Institute for Christian Resources and long-time singles specialist, estimates that it takes approximately two years for a single parent to recover to the point where he/she can be a productive member of the church. In other words, when adults go through a divorce crisis and are forced to "begin over again," they will likely be "consumers" when they come to the church, rather than "givers." One of the tasks to accomplish is "welfare weaning"; that is, helping single moms get free of the welfare system (emotionally and physically) and become established in their new lives. These people need to meet and talk with other single parents for support. They need caring church leadership to provide guidance and (most importantly) encouragement. As church leaders, we would do well to take the admonition of James concerning widows and orphans (James 1:27) and apply it to those within today's society who are disenfranchised, alienated, and vulnerable.

Last, but certainly not least, is the issue of spiritual life development. I place this at the end of the list because today's single adult must struggle with this area in the midst of the previous six areas of concern. At times it seems as though one or another of these concerns overshadows or completely displaces the spiritual; however, this is often just the surface appearance, or at least merely a temporary phase. Most single people that I meet have a genuine interest in spiritual life issues. They want to know how to be a Christian, how to translate the Bible into modern life situations, and how to fit into the church. On the other hand, numerous single adults have dismissed the church and the Bible as

[15]*U.S. News and World Report,* June 1985, p. 63.

being irrelevant to their needs and their world. Here, the church leader must develop the "missionary mentality" which asks the question, "How can I translate Christianity into this foreign culture?" When we take this approach, the results can be truly exciting!

To speak about single adults and single adult ministry is also to speak of modern society in the midst of far-reaching trends and changes. It is a complex picture once a person moves from the place of casual observer to that of student. But move we must if we are to keep a grasp upon the times in which we live. The primary thesis of this book is that the church of Jesus Christ *can* make a difference in the variegated lives of today's single people. This is not to say that every congregation should have or strive to have a formal ministry to singles. Some congregations will be good at one approach; others will be good at something else. Regardless of what some of today's "mega-churches" would like us to think—no *one* church can do it all! However, it is also true that every congregation can do something.

For the purpose of analysis we can say that there are essentially five "response levels" which characterize the local church regarding single adult ministry. *Level One* could be described as a "non-ministry" response. Churches that fall into this category may very well be healthy and active in their community, and they may also have a number of single adults within their general membership. However, this type of church sees no distinction between single adults and any other kind of adult. No acknowledgement is offered concerning their existence or presence in the church. They are simply lumped together with everyone else and expected to fit in somehow. I use the term "non-ministry" here not to imply that the singles in this type of church will not hear the gospel or learn of the salvation of Christ—but to say that there exists no "directed" ministry toward the single person.

On *Level Two* a church, particularly its leaders, is very much aware of the single adults' presence and there is genuine concern; however, this church is unable to create any formal type of program for its single people.

The difference between this level and Level One has to do not only in regard to awareness, but specifically in regard to attitude and response. A Level Two ministry is one in which the leaders, especially the minister, work to develop an *atmosphere of acknowledgement and acceptance* for the single person. By means of public remarks from the pulpit ("God loves single people and so do we!") and personal words of encouragement (e.g. an elder approaches a single person and says, "I know we don't have any special programs to offer singles, but we're glad you're here and we want to help"). This type of church does minister to the single, and it is very much appreciated!

A significant change takes place at *Level Three.* Whereas on Level Two the ministry to singles took the form of attitudes, acknowledgements, and atmosphere—now it shows itself in organizational activity. On Level Three church leaders participate in various ways to facilitate the development of a *program.* Examples of this would be an elder hosting a social activity in his home; a minister meeting with a small group of singles to discuss possibilities for growth; a church classroom being offered to the singles for a Bible study; the newsletter carrying an endorsement for the group from an elder or minister; or the minister helping the group put together a seminar for singles. Many churches function on this level and a lot can be accomplished by this approach.

Level Four marks the beginning of the "formal program" phase of development. On this level actual staff time is allocated for singles ministry as well as some means of financing the program.

Level Five continues this development with the employment of a distinct staff person (at least half-time status) plus a formal budget allotment. By this point the single adult ministry is a well-defined, well-supported, and easily-recognized part of the overall church ministry. I would estimate that about five percent of the total number of churches today have developed a Level Five ministry.

Over the last 10 years I have discussed single adult

ministry with ministers of all ages and from various parts of the country. Among other questions, I have often asked, "Why doesn't your church minister to single adults, particularly those beyond the college years?" The answers I have received to that question have been varied; however there seems to be essentially seven major reasons (apart from laziness or ignorance) why churches do not reach out to this growing and needy segment of America:

1) *Budget.* "We just don't have the necessary financial resources to develop a special ministry."

2) *Ministry Priority.* Many ministers follow a traditional priority list when it comes to selecting staff and programs. This list usually goes something like this: preaching minister, education minister, youth or music minister, children's minister, evangelism minister ... and then *maybe* a singles minister ... maybe.

3) *Lack of Single People.* Some churches operate in communities where few, if any, singles dwell. Why start a ministry if no one can use it?

4) *Past Failures.* "We tried that once and it was a dismal failure—so we quit. Singles work is not for us!"

5) *Fear.* Many church leaders believe that to open the church doors to the singles of America would be tantamount to the opening of Pandora's Box. The church could be flooded with "swinging singles," those with the "divorce disease," and other worldly elements.

6) *Theological Concerns.* One minister told me that his church did not offer a ministry to those who were "single again" because it would draw the divorced. His position was that a ministry for these people would be catering to those in sin and, by implication, condoning divorce.

7) *Family Ministry Philosophy.* This position holds that the church should design its ministry for families and that to do otherwise would serve to undermine the already weakened family structure in America today.

As was stated earlier in this chapter, it is certainly not this author's position that every church should have a formal singles ministry. None of us can do everything ... but all of us can do something! And, although the seven reasons for non-involvement listed above may sound reasonable on the surface, they will not stand up to close and honest scrutiny (except perhaps number three). Not all levels of ministry require budget support in order to be effective (cf. Levels One and Two); although staff and program development must follow careful and prayerful prioritization—this does not mean that the "traditional way" is the only acceptable pattern! A good dose of creativity could solve this problem. Past failures at any ministry project can be disappointing, but it does not need to be debilitating. And, regarding theological concerns, it is true that as church leaders, we must guard the truth—but we must be careful lest we end up guarding the truth but fail to guard the flock God has entrusted to us. If Jesus had chosen to minister *only* to those who were in right standing with the church and in compliance with Biblical doctrine, He would never have reached out to the Gentiles, tax collectors, harlots, terrorists, and ... you and me.

Finally, the family ministry excuse is just that—an excuse. We need to redefine the commonly held family idea and go beyond "nuclear family" to "the family of God." In the final analysis, we are not just talking about "singles"; we are talking about people who stand in need of the salvation of Jesus Christ. If we ever reach a position where we have developed reasons to exclude them from our ministries, then our reasoning has gone too far.

CHAPTER TWO

About This Chapter's Author

Terry Fisher

Terry Fisher is a minister, singer, songwriter, storyteller, guitarist, husband, and father. He graduated from the Cincinnati Bible College in 1977 with a B.A. in Christian Ministries. For fourteen years, beginning in 1971, he was on the staff of the Jesus House, a coffee house and concert ministry that was located in Cincinnati, Ohio. Since November, 1983, he has served on the Youth and Young Adult staff of College Hill Presbyterian church, Cincinnati, Ohio. One of his primary responsibilities during that time has been Ambassadors For Christ, the Career Age Single Adult Ministry. He has also spent time traveling as a concert performer and seminar speaker. A songbook of original songs has been published by Music Lab Publication, Cincinnati, Ohio.

–2–

Starting or Reviving a Single Adult Ministry

by Terry Fisher

In the spring of 1972, eight people in Cincinnati, Ohio, began meeting together for a weekly Bible study. At the conclusion of their initial six-week commitment, they decided to continue meeting. As they began inviting others, the numbers began to increase until they had outgrown the basement in which they were meeting. The host couple decided to buy a new house with a bigger basement. With the new location, the numbers continued to increase until that space was outgrown. A different meeting location was found in the library of a local high school. The group, known as "College & Careers," continued to meet there until 1976 when it was placed under the supervision of College Hill Presbyterian Church and began meeting on the church property.

Today, the group is known as "Ambassadors for Christ," the career-age (ages 22-30) single adult fellowship at College Hill Presbyterian Church. Attendance is 80 to 100 at the weekly meeting, which is a time of worship, teaching, small group sharing, and prayer. "Ambassadors" ministers not just to singles of CHPC, but to singles from all over Greater Cincinnati. In a poll taken in the spring of 1985, 50% of the group were members of other congregations. Forty different churches were represented. This is the current status of the group that started as a small group Bible study. A singles fellowship made up of single adults from several church groups was not the original vision of that study, but this is an example of God's doing more than was originally envisioned.

Barry Tucker, on the staff at the First Church of Christ, Florence, Kentucky, was given the task of starting a singles ministry at First Church. For the first meeting, he decided to organize a cookout on the church property. To communicate this, he had announcements made from the pulpit, wrote an article for the church newsletter, included announcements in the Sunday worship guide, and contacted people one-on-one. Twenty-three people attended the cookout. The age range was 22 to 58. Barry made strategic use of name tags to eliminate the embarrassment of members of the same congregation not knowing one another's names. Most of the time was spent eating and talking. After the meal, they had a short devotion, then discussed the needs and wants of the people, concluding the discussion with the formation of a leadership team. The discussion led them to several conclusions regarding their future format. The group did not express a need for many planned social activities, but had some other specific needs. First, they decided to keep the various age groups together, seeing the differences in ages as a strength, at the same time acknowledging that natural age divisions may occur at a later date. Second, they decided to meet weekly on Sunday mornings at a local restaurant for breakfast and a short teaching. Afterwards they would attend the regular Sunday worship service. Their third idea was to keep in touch during the week on a one-to-one basis. They intended to pass out names each Sunday and call one another mid-week to offer personal encouragement.

"Jericho Road Ministries," the singles ministry of East 91st Street Christian Church in Indianapolis, Indiana, has a Sunday-school class which numbers 150. In addition, they host a once-a-month Christian music concert which attracts 300. Most of these singles are in their twenties and thirties although they do have some involvement from people who are 40 to 50 years old. They have a leadership team which oversees 20 ministry areas: follow-up of visitors, service within the church, service outside the church, evangelistic outreach projects, retreats and seminars, prayer, coffee houses, sports, etc. As recent as 1984, they had a struggling ministry of 15 to 20 single adults meeting for a Sunday-school class. The difference was the result of one man having a vision of an active, thriving singles ministry. He was not on the staff of the church; he was one of the single adults in the struggling Sunday-school class. Believing that there could be a stronger singles ministry occurring, he called an organizational meeting for anyone who had an interest. Twenty-five people attended. Six of those committed themselves to accepting leadership responsibilities. They started weekly small groups, Tuesday evening volleyball, and getting together one Saturday night a month at a coffee house. The Sunday-school class was the weekly hub—as new people attended one of the other activities, they were invited to the Sunday-school class. The leadership team grew to 12 members, more small groups were added, and attendance began to increase at the social activities. Momentum built and J.R.M. grew into what it is today.

Describe your congregation. Is it large or small? Are the members in their twenties and thirties or is most of the congregation over fifty? Is it in the inner city or a rural setting? Is it surrounded by colleges?

There are two classifications which are used to help identify congregations. The categories are "urban" and "rural." These categories have little to do with location—they mostly identify type and style of congregations. Urban congregations are usually interested in growing in numbers because they want as many people as possible involved in the church. They are ready to try something new. They are ready to do as many things as possible. This type of congregation tends to be large in numbers and possesses many different ministry opportunities.

The rural congregations tend to want to remain small in numbers. Everyone likes to know everyone else. The tendency is toward being a close-knit family. This type of congregation usually remains small in numbers and tends to focus on one or two ministry opportunities.

Both types of congregations are good. They can both

be places where Christians can grow spiritually. The importance behind identifying the type is the help it will give in determining what type of singles ministry can be started in your congregation.

Here are more questions for you to consider: what about neighboring congregations? Are they small or large? Are they following the Lord or following traditions or maintaining status quo? How about the community? Is it a growing suburban area or a decaying section of town which is losing its residents?

Honest answers will indicate both limitations and potential for singles ministry. From them a starting point will be derived. It is hard to know what directions a ministry will travel, but it is good to have a starting point. If the congregation is small, the singles ministry will start small and may remain small. If a neighboring congregation has a large singles ministry, use that as a resource. Very often, small singles groups visit "Ambassadors" in Cincinnati and participate in one of the meetings or social activities. If your congregation is large, you may be the people who could provide the funds and staffing for a community-wide singles fellowship in which others could participate while maintaining involvement in their home churches. Your congregation should be willing to make a commitment of finances to the singles ministry although by no means should it be completely supported in this way. The singles involved in the ministry should be given the opportunity to support the program financially. Members of College Hill Presbyterian Church who are involved in "Ambassadors" can designate funds to an account which is used to pay for some of the programs. These donations are encouraged to be over and above regular giving to the congregation.

What is the best type of singles ministry? Is it one that emphasizes prayer and Bible study? Should it encourage dating and marriage? Are weekly social gatherings necessary? What about lots of teaching on the struggles of being single?

The best type of singles ministry is one that is effective. Success is not determined by numbers or type of program. An effective singles ministry is one that meets the needs of singles and spurs them on to spiritual and emotional maturity. Helpful guidelines are found in Scripture such as these in Colossians 1:28 and Hebrews 10:24, 25 (NIV):

"We proclaim him, admonishing and teaching everyone with all wisdom, so that we may present everyone perfect in Christ . . .
And let us consider how we may spur one another on toward love and good deeds. Let us not give up meeting together, as some are in the habit of doing, but let us encourage one another—and all the more as you see the Day approaching."

Amy called on the phone wanting to know if the church had anything for college students. She was attending a local college, visited the church one Sunday, and attended a Sunday-school class for singles. She did not know that the class was intended for people who were 30 and older. She listened to people share their struggles of being divorced, widowed, single parents. She left the class depressed! Her response was, "I'm too young to be single. Don't you have anything for college students?"

Amy's experience shows that there are very different needs among the groups which could be included in the broad category of "single adult." The normal divisions are as follows:

- 18 to 22 years old: college students and non-student college age
- 22 to 35 years old: career-age single adults
- 30 to 50 years old: older singles

At College Hill Presbyterian Church these are three different ministries. The 18-to 22-year-old category is people right out of high school starting college or jobs. The 22-to 35-year-old category is "Ambassadors For Christ." Those who are 30 to 50 years of age constitute a group known as "Mosaics." These people include a large number of divorced and widowed. The needs of the groups are very different. The types of programming will need to be adjusted to meet those needs.

There is a lot of variety in format which is being used in this type of ministry. One ministry can model a lot of format variety. "Ambassadors For Christ" has several different types of meetings. Sunday night is the large group meeting. It lasts two hours and consists of worship, teaching, small group discussion, and prayer. Once a month this format is changed to what the group calls a Body Life Meeting. On this particular night, the meeting may consist of a concert, a missions presentation, a performance by a theatrical troupe, or simply an extended time of praise and worship.

Besides the Sunday-night meetings, there are three social gatherings per month. Two of these are held in homes and are called Fellowships. The host provides the place; everyone who attends provides the refreshments. The third event each month is a social activity. This is a planned activity which usually costs money to attend. In the past, the group has attended baseball games, enjoyed catered dinners, gone to dances, and taken a riverboat cruise. Once they invaded a local drive-in and dominated several rows. One winter the activity was extended over a weekend as the group drove to Gatlinburg, Tennessee, for a "Cabin Fever Weekend."

"Ambassadors" also has a small group network. These are held in homes on a weekly basis and are Bible studies or support groups or both. This is something we encourage people to do if they are not already involved in small groups at their churches.

Of all the things which "Ambassadors" offers, the most highly attended function is the Sunday-evening meeting. The main reason is because it is regular and weekly. For "Ambassadors," this is the hub.

The best way to start this type of ministry and find out the interest level is to have an organizational meeting. The objectives for this meeting are threefold: 1) to allow people an opportunity to get acquainted; 2) to discuss the needs, desires, and expectations of a single adult ministry; and 3) to establish leadership. Five things will help these goals be achieved: 1) a comfortable location; 2) name tags; 3) food; 4) games; and 5) discussion time.

It does not matter if the location of this meeting is at the church building or in someone's home, as long as the people are comfortable. If you decide on a home, make sure the host understands that disruptions by pets or children need to be controlled.

The name tags are important because, regardless of the size of the group, someone will not know someone, or even worse, someone will know someone but will have forgotten the name. That can cause embarrassment!

Food is important because food is important. Every Sunday at noon restaurants all over America are invaded by massive quantities of Christians eating massive quantities of food. Refreshments help people feel comfortable. They prime the conversation pump. A full meal is not necessary; some creative desserts or appetizers are sufficient. Serve something creative and have the recipe handy. As you plan the food, remember, this is a weight-conscious age in time.

If any get-acquainted games are planned, keep in mind this is not a youth group. These are adults. There are lots of fun games to use during which people can maintain their dignity. The following are two 10-question quizzes which are effective for getting acquainted. Pass out paper and pens. After the quiz has been taken, have people share answers in a large or small group setting.

Quiz Number One

People Are Strange

1. Where do you squeeze the toothpaste tube?
2. How often do you dust the furniture?
3. When and how often do you wash clothes?
4. When do you clean your apartment or house?
5. Who maintains your automobile?
6. How many books have you read in the last month?
7. If you were to buy a new stereo, would you save the

money or charge it?

8. Do you buy books or check them out of the library?
9. How many records or tapes have you bought in the last year?
10. Do you buy only Christian music, only secular music, or both?

Quiz Number Two

Are You Living in Suspended Animation?

Answer "yes" or "no" to the following questions.

1. Did you take at least one week of vacation last year apart from visiting family members?
2. Have you celebrated any major holidays (i.e. Christmas, Thanksgiving, etc.) at some place other than your parents' house?
3. Have you ceased to refer to visiting your parents as "going home"?
4. Do you sleep on a real bed instead of a mattress on the floor?
5. If you wanted to see a movie, but couldn't find anyone to see it with you, would you see it alone?
6. Is your house or apartment decorated in a way which reflects your creativity and personality?
7. Do you cook real meals? (As opposed to cold soup out of the can ...)
8. Have you registered to vote in the next election?
9. Are you content enough to remain single for the next ten years?
10. Are you saving money?

If you answered "yes" to at least seven of the questions, you are doing a good job of living in the real world. Answering four to six "yes's" is not bad but you are missing a lot in life. Three or fewer "yes's" sounds like you are sitting home waiting for marriage to happen to you!

46

Hopefully, this meeting is planned on an evening where the food and get-acquainted time will occupy only the first part. The rest of the evening can be given over to the task at hand. Allow everyone the opportunity to introduce himself to the whole group. This should be a brief introduction, just the basic facts: name, place of employment, and something interesting about himself. After these introductions, begin discussing the needs and wants of the group. Let the future format of the group flow out of those needs. The group may be like the Florence people and not have many needs for social interaction. Find out who is willing to accept responsibilities for organizing the format. Establish a means for future communication, such as a newsletter or announcement sheet, and have someone accept that responsibility.

It is very likely that during this initial discussion, or very soon after, the issue will arise concerning a name for the group. People like to have identifying tags. There is nothing wrong with that. Choosing a name can be lots of fun and can give an opportunity for creative expression. The following are some standard names which are used a lot by single adult groups:

Ambassadors For Christ—Taken from 2 Corinthians 5:20

F.O.C.A.S.—Fellowship Of Caring Adult Singles

S.P.L.A.S.H.—Single People Loving And Serving Him

M.O.S.A.I.C.S.—Ministry Of Single Adults In Christ's Service

These are great names, but they are given to stimulate your thinking. Let the group create a new one. It helps give ownership to the ministry. The results may be surprising. One college fellowship named themselves "Hoshen." It was a newly created word, not an acrostic, did not mean anything, but they loved it!

This first meeting is a springboard. Implement the good ideas as quickly as possible. Help those who have volunteered for leadership to understand their responsibilities. If a staff person is to oversee or lead the group, make sure this person's responsibilities are very clear.

The bulk of the leadership should come from the group. Any staff person should be a resource to those leaders. Have a great first meeting—and don't forget the name tags!

You may find yourself in a position of deciding what to do with an already existing singles group. This poses a different dilemma when faced with the prospect of trying to revive a dead singles group. Should time and money be invested in attempting to resurrect something which the Lord may intend to leave dead? The decision is best made by the leadership of your congregation. If the decision is to try reviving, be encouraged—it is not an impossible task.

In November, 1983, I was hired by College Hill Presbyterian Church to lead "Ambassadors for Christ." Three weeks before starting the job, I visited one of the Sunday-evening meetings. At the time, very few people knew I was to be the new leader, so I was able to visit as a normal new person. I left the meeting with one impression: it was boring! I understood why attendance was so bad. The group size had diminished in the previous few years, dropping from 100 members to 25. As I started the job, several people approached me and shared their impression that the group was dead. They wanted to know if I agreed! This was not the most encouraging way to start a new job. The truth was, I agreed with them, but I saw signs of life that encouraged me. I was convinced that "Ambassadors" still had lots of potential.

I have always been amazed at our ability to make things boring. Sunday-morning worship services, Bible studies, and prayer meetings all have a general reputation for being boring. Those which are not boring are considered surprising exceptions. This is one of the reasons why we have such a difficult time persuading non-Christians to visit church. Whose fault is it when church is boring? Is God at fault? No! There is nothing boring about God. The Bible presents us with a creative God who established a world full of variety and change. He creates us to be people of creativity. We often take His creativity, think of a new idea, evaluate it as a good idea, use it, abuse it, and turn it into a tradition from which we never deviate. The tradition soon loses its meaning and becomes a boring religious activity. We defend its use on the basis of tradition, which is a weak defense. The God of the Bible is not a God of tradition. He is a God of change, a God who is ready to do something new and unexpected.

Just before my arrival, "Ambassadors" had begun making changes which were aimed at reviving. Two of these were the adoption of a new name and an alteration in the teaching content at the large group meeting.

From its inception, "Ambassadors" had been called "College and Careers." The original focus of the group had been on people who were out of high school and in the midst of college or some type of job. Over the years, the age group had continued to be older people. Many college and career groups cater to people who are 18 to 22 years of age and are either in college or have bypassed college and begun a career. "Ambassadors" had begun to attract more and more people who were in their mid to late twenties. There were very few college age people attending the group. In recognizing this, the leadership felt the name was misleading, thus the change. Like many changes, it was not a completely smooth transition. Some people were upset that the leadership would be so bold. Any time tradition—any tradition—is confronted, there is the potential of people being hurt or upset. The result could be the loss of those individuals. Some of these people found it necessary to discontinue involvement.

"Ambassadors" also had a tradition of topical teachings at the large group meetings. The leadership decided to change this format to one which involved teaching through a book of the Bible, a chapter per week. It was felt that this would give a more Biblical base to the teaching time and give a better opportunity at meeting the different maturity levels of those in attendance.

After my arrival, the reviving continued in two interrelated areas: the atmosphere of the Sunday meetings, and leadership development.

49

A leader sets the tone of a meeting. If he wants, he can infuse it with enthusiasm and creativity. The worship and teaching times at the "Ambassador" meetings needed to exhibit these attributes. That was my focus for the first three months. Every time I led worship or taught, I consciously tried to interject these elements into what I did. My intention was to be a spark and encourage others to do the same. This was a very visible expression of something new for the group. It attracted a lot of attention which resulted in a higher attendance at the meetings. Regardless of that, it was not the most important element in the reviving.

The most important thing which occurred was the leadership development. This is illustrated in the experiences of three of the men in the group; Jerry, Steve, and Gus.

Jerry had become a Christian through his involvement with "Ambassadors." He had been actively involved with the group for several years and was on the leadership team when I began working with them. He was also on the search committee which hired me. Jerry was one of the few people in the group who was willing to share in the teaching responsibilities. Because of his interest and willingness, I encouraged him to teach more often. We began meeting together to help him develop this talent. Each time he taught, we met to evaluate the teaching. He was an example to others in the group. This example stimulated them to teach. Soon, enough teachers were raised up so that 50% of the teaching was done by people from the group. Even people who have been hesitant to teach alone have been able to participate. When "Ambassadors" studied Joshua, one of the small groups assumed the responsibility of teaching chapter six, the fall of Jericho. They presented it as a news report with members of the small group portraying the characters from the chapter.

Steve began at "Ambassadors" the same night I did. Word spread around the group that he was a proficient guitarist. I asked him to help me lead worship at one of the meetings. He agreed, did a wonderful job, but claims to have been scared to death. That was the beginning. He gained an interest in the area of worship, began studying the subject, and taught others what he learned. He soon assumed the leadership team position of worship coordinator. Under his guidance, many more people were trained as worship leaders. Utilizing his creativity, he planned nights of worship which focused on special themes. "Psalm 150 Night" was an evening when everyone brought instruments and played during worship. On "John Michael Talbot Night," all of the worship songs were those written by John Michael Talbot. "Jewish Music Night" incorporated Hebrew Christian music. For this night, Steve invited dancers from a local Hebrew Christian congregation who taught us Jewish folk dances they used during worship.

Because of the rapid growth, "Ambassadors" was faced with a strange dilemma: there were many people who wanted to be involved in a small support group, but there was a lack of trained leaders. At the time, small groups were led and hosted by the same person. That is a lot of responsibility. A suggestion arose: why not let two people share the responsibility? One person can host, and the other can lead. Gus agreed to lead, but only to help the small group get started. He had never led anything like that before. We met together to brainstorm and evaluate ideas for small groups. Gus led a very strong group. As a result of that experience, a year later he accepted the leadership team responsibility as small group coordinator. He was instrumental in helping others get involved in small groups. As a resource to help "Ambassadors" learn about small groups, he organized two small group conferences.

This type of leadership, from within the group, is a key to an effective singles ministry. Too often people rely on the youth ministry model of recruiting a couple from the church to lead a singles ministry. This is not necessary. I believe it is a hindrance. A singles ministry is a ministry to adults. They do not need to be led by married volunteers. They can and will do a better job of being responsible for themselves.

Whether you are starting a new singles ministry or reviving an old one, I hope these ideas will be of practical help. Be ready for the Lord to do something new and unexpected through you.

Bibliography

U.S. News & World Report, February 21, 1983, "19 Million Singles, Their Joys and Frustrations"
Group Magazine, November 1983
Leadership Magazine, Fall Quarter, 1983
Stories of Significant Young Adult Ministries, Allen W. Kratz, printed by the United Presbyterian Church, USA. 475 Riverside Dr., Room 1164, N.Y., NY 10115

Newsletter Resources

Single Adult Ministries Journal, published ten times per year, a publication of Solo Ministries, P.O. Box 1408, Sisters, OR 97759
Single Heart Journal, published by Nancy Honeytree, P.O. Box 175, Fort Wayne, IN 46801
The Small Group Newsletter, not specifically a singles publication, P.O. Box 6000, Colorado Springs, CO 80934
Young Adult Ministries, published by the Young Calvinist Federation, 1333 Alger S.E., Box 7259, Grand Rapids, MI 49510
Servant, "A publication challenging all singles to serve Christ," published by Mobilized To Serve, a ministry sponsored by Elim Fellowship, 7245 College St., Lima, NY 14485
The SAM Network, a bulletin board for ministers/leaders involved in single adult ministry, P.O. Box 1408, Sisters, OR 97759

CHAPTER THREE

About This Chapter's Author

Krista Swan Welsh

Krista Swan Welsh is Editor of Junior Age Vacation Bible School Materials at Standard Publishing. She graduated from The Cincinnati Bible College in 1983 with a B. S. in Christian Education and Journalism. Her church work experience has included teaching several different age groups, singing, playing trumpet and French horn, writing skits for church programs, and serving on various committees.

Before her marriage in 1986, Krista spent much of her time serving with "Fellowship," a single adult ministry at Clovernook Christian Church in Cincinnati, Ohio. While in that group she served one year as President.

Today Krista spends most of her free time working on writing projects and enjoying time with her family.

—3—

Let's Get Organized!
Determining Group Structure

by Krista Swan Welsh

The first week in May, 1983, probably holds the record for being the most transitional week in my life. I graduated from college and found a new apartment that Friday, placed my church membership in a new congregation on Sunday, and started working at a new job on Monday. Whew!

There were a lot of new beginnings for me then, which is bound to be scary for anyone. I was thankful that a few months before that hectic time, I had found new friends in a single adult Sunday-school class at Clovernook Christian Church in Cincinnati. The class was called "Fellowship," and it was largely due to their outreach that helped my decision to join that congregation.

Things were really starting to take off with "Fellowship" then. I became very active in their many get-togethers. In 1984 I was selected to serve as class president and therefore got to have a part in the organizational end of this ministry. We experimented with many different ways of organizing a single adult ministry. Hopefully, my sharing this organization will help you in your ministry to single adults.

Begin at the Beginning

Before determining organization, establish a pur-

55

pose. Why does your group exist? Make a list. Here is a sample:

The purpose of the existence of a single adult ministry in our church is to help single adults grow:
1) in their personal lives
2) in their social lives
3) in their ministries

This can be a starting point. Now let's break it down a little more than that.

Helping Single Adults Grow in Their Personal Lives

Sunday School

This is a great base. As I mentioned earlier, I became an active member of "Fellowship" after first attending their Sunday-school class. Singles looking for fellowship with other Christians may look here first. Provide good topics of study. See chapter four in this book.

Bible Study

An informal time of sharing, discussing, and learning is also important in the lives of single adults. Your group needs to decide whether it is best for them to meet once a week, once every other week, or whatever. Again, see chapter four in this book for good Bible-study topics.

Prayer Partners

This is a great way to form strong, one-on-one friendships. Having a prayer partner means you have someone you can always confidentially go to with prayer requests, and vice versa. When "Fellowship" did this, we simply let everyone select one partner of their choice. We did ask everyone to choose a partner that was of the same sex, because it is generally easier to confide in someone of the same sex, but again, set guidelines according to YOUR group. We also asked the partners to meet at least once a week to pray together, either in person or on the phone.

Library

Make sure your church has good resources for single adults. If they don't, help them develop a good library for single adults, or start one in your Sunday-school classroom. See the "Resources" pages at the end of this book for ideas.

Special Seminars

Personal testimonies are often interesting and helpful here. Know of a single parent who is successfully running a Christian home for his or her family? Have that person come and talk with your singles. We (the leadership) also hosted speakers who talked with our class about budgeting, self-esteem, problem solving, spiritual gifts, and goal-setting.

Helping Single Adults Grow in Their Social Lives

When I was single and lived on my own, I really dreaded two things: 1) eating alone; and 2) not having anything to do or anywhere to go on Friday nights. "Fellowship" helped me avoid those two areas.

Eat Out Together

Traditions are important in families; so it is in your single adult class "family." The "Fellowship" class enjoyed a tradition of going out to eat lunch every Sunday after church. Often we ate in a restaurant, or every once in a while someone from the group hosted the whole gang in his or her home. Smaller groups of us often met for supper before going to evening worship together.

Class Parties and Class Meetings

"Fellowship" met the third Friday evening of every month for our class meeting. We met in our Sunday-school teachers' home, and took turns bringing refreshments and games. What goes on at a class meeting? We used this time to cover class business, as well as have a little fun. Class meetings were also times to bring in special speakers.

Flocks

This was another name we gave "small groups." In addition to getting together as one big happy group, we also divided into groups of eight to twelve people, which met for close, informal times. It may have been getting together for dinner and a show, or just sitting on someone's living room floor and sharing thoughts for a few hours. Each flock had a flock leader, who was responsible for planning flock get-togethers.

Helping Single Adults Grow in Their Ministries

This is where detailed organization really comes into the picture. Single adults have many ministries in which to serve. We divided into committees, according to our ministry desires. Our categories can hopefully serve as an example for you.

Inreach Committee

Members of this committee were responsible for ministering to the members of the "Fellowship" class. This committee prepared a class prayer chain, and alerted other class members when a fellow class member needed prayer in any way. They also alerted the class whenever a class member needed help in any way: finding a new job, finding a new residence, moving, giving support when a relative was sick or had died.

Outreach Committee

Members of this committee were an extension of the church evangelism team. Follow-up on guests and visitors was the main emphasis, through cards, phone calls, personal visits.

Activities Committee

Members of this committee were responsible for monthly class activities. They prepared an activities calendar two months in advance and presented this calendar at the monthly class meeting for approval, changes, and additions. They were also responsible for making reservations when necessary, planning menus for these activities when necessary, gathering information regarding costs.

Bible-Study/Sunday-School Materials Committee

Members of this committee were responsible for gathering and presenting at class meetings a variety of topics, materials, and resources of specific study subjects. They were also responsible for contacting and reserving special study leaders and teachers.

Communications Committee

Members of this committee were responsible for compiling, publishing, and circulating a monthly class newsletter; compiling, publishing and circulating a class address, birthday, and phone number list (update every four to six months, depending on the number of changes); and making sure class events were published in the church bulletin and weekly newsletter. "Fellowship's" monthly newsletter was called "Body Builder," and featured: a monthly calendar which noted upcoming class events (work with Activities Committee on this), a devotional editorial, news about class members, a prayer request list, address and phone number changes, reports on past class activities, and a variety of special features. Seek out members of your class who have design experience, writing experience, access to a good electric typewriter or word processor, access to art, and access to copying machines. The newsletter doesn't *have* to be anything fancy; it does have to communicate effectively. The "Body Builder" started small (one 8½" x 14" piece of paper, typed on both sides and mimeographed on the church machinery) and grew. Within a few months, "Body Builder" was one or two 8½" x 14" pieces of paper (sometimes colored), folded in half to an attractive 7" x 8½" layout. We were fortunate to have access to clip art, an excellent copier, and a word processor that automatically justified margins.

Mission/Service Projects Committee

Members of this committee were responsible for examining possible mission projects and presenting them to the class for approval. This can include monetary support and/or becoming involved with a physical need. "Fellowship" spent much of their time helping a handicapped lady named Ellie (name has been changed). Ellie, who lived alone, was in a wheelchair and unable to get out of her home by herself. Members of "Fellowship" took turns taking Ellie shopping, giving her rides to church, or just telephoning her occasionally to talk. One sunny Autumn afternoon an ambitious group of "Fellowshippers" went to Ellie's house and completely cleaned it. This group also held a cookout in Ellie's front yard that day, and enjoyed Ellie's company.

These committees work ideally if your class has committed, dependable members. It is often hard work, is not always fun fulfilling the responsibilities one has agreed to undertake, but it certainly is valuable to the service of Christ.

Another way of organizing class responsibilities is by electing or appointing class officers. A "Class Officers' Duties Description" could read as follows:

President:

1. Make announcements every Sunday morning (including prayer praises and requests) or make arrangements with the Vice President to do so.
2. Meet twice a month with teachers and other officers to discuss class business. (We met every other Sunday afternoon.)
3. Call class meetings and inform the class when and where they are to meet.
4. Greet and welcome all new visitors and keep in contact with new members, visitors and key church members.
5. Be the motivator (enthusiastic) for all class activities and duties (Communion clean-up, Sunday-morning greeters, Communion visitation, etc.)
6. Be concerned with and informed of individual problems within the class and of any that will affect the class and let appropriate people know of these.
7. Keep officers and class teachers informed.
8. Be liason between class members, officers, teachers and church.
9. Be in attendance at all class functions if possible.
10. Be ready to represent the class at church functions.

Vice President:

1. Represent the president whenever he/she is absent, such as in Sunday school, class meetings, class socials, etc.
2. Assist the president whenever needed.
3. Keep the flock leaders informed of their duties and pass along pertinent information to them.
4. Assign visitors and new members to flock leaders and keep the secretary informed of this.
5. Greet and welcome any new visitor.

Secretaries (We had two; they split the responsibilities):

1. Make sure all class members receive the monthly class newsletter. Keep a file of extra newsletters.
2. Send birthday, sympathy, congratulations (or whatever applies) cards to class participants.
3. Have new visitors fill out new visitors cards. Keep record of these and then pass to appropriate persons (Outreach Committee).
4. Write notes to all visitors.
5. Keep minutes of class meetings.
6. Greet and welcome all visitors.
7. Inform church office about class activities every Sunday.
8. Be responsible for weekly class offering.
9. Keep attendance records for Sunday school.
10. Greet and welcome all new visitors.
11. Prepare and present secretarial and treasurer's report to other class officers at meetings twice a month.

Flock Leaders (Small Group Leaders)

1. Keep other class officers informed of class members' needs.
2. Plan flock get-togethers.

62

3. Call all persons in your group to inform about class activities and flock get-togethers.
4. Get to know your group personally, through phone calls, personal visits, class activities, flock get-togethers.

NOTE: Some of the officers' responsibilities may overlap with those of the committees'. You have the choice to decide what will work best for your single adult group, and divide the responsibilities accordingly.

CHAPTER FOUR

About This Chapter's Author

Gerald Denny

Gerald Denny is presently serving as minister of the Champaign-Urbana Christian Church in Illinois. For two years he served as minister of education for churches in Clinton, Illinois; Decatur, Georgia; and Terre Haute, Indiana. He has worked closely with single adult ministries during those years, taking the initiative to begin several Bible-school and weeknight classes for adult singles as well as support groups for widows.

Gerald received the A. B. Degree in Ministerial Science from Lincoln Christian College, the M. A. Degree in New Testament from Lincoln Christian Seminary, and the M. Ed. Degree in Educational Psychology from the University of Illinois.

—4—

What Single Adults Like to Study: Ideas for Bible Study and Sunday School

by Gerald Denny

Single adults are as varied as single snowflakes. In discovering what they like to study some of the basic differences in their circumstances and attitudes first need to be acknowledged.

Differences in Circumstances

Marital Experience

There are adults who have never been married. These can be subdivided into those who have deliberately chosen a lifetime of singleness for the sake of the gospel (1 Corinthians 7:32-38), those who are at peace with their singleness but who are open to the possibility of marriage, and those who are eager and desirous for marriage.

Then there are adults who have experienced the death of their marriage partner. Some even have gone through this painful loss more than once. For some it was after many years together.

There are also adults who have been divorced. Again, some have gone through this difficult experience more than once. Some were married only briefly. Others were married for years. Some may be soured on the possibility of any future marriage. Others may yearn to remarry as soon as possible.

Children

Some single adults may be "never married" mothers or fathers. Others may be parents who were formerly married.

The number of children may vary from one to six or more. One single adult may have a new baby and a 10-year-old. Another may have a grade-schooler and two teenagers. Still another may have grown children with families of their own.

Children under college age may be living with the former spouse or the grandparents. On the other hand, they may rarely see the former spouse. Then again, they may be in the middle of a power struggle between a set of divorced parents.

Age

When is a person considered an adult? Some say at age 18; others, at age 21. Thus, the age range for single adults is 18 or 21 and up.

Usually, when speaking of single adults, a more limited age range is being considered (e.g. 25 to 55). But the needs of single adults on either side of that range must not be ignored.

More and more people are living to 70, 80, and 90 years of age. Most are mentally alert and physically able to continue learning in Bible-school classes or home study groups. This writer has an 89-year-old aunt who is a widow. She goes twice a week to continuing education classes at a local state university. She is also very active in her Sunday-morning Bible-school class and her monthly women's circle meeting.

Of course, the millions of college-age single adults should also be of special concern in church programming and ministry. College is a major time for solidifying values for oneself and making key decisions that will affect the rest of one's life.

Interests

Because of the varying work responsibilities, personal skills, hobbies, and past experiences to be found among single adults, some topics for study will have much more appeal to some than to others.

The most pressing concern for some may be how to keep their ethical integrity in the non-Christian business world. For others, it may be the resolving of interpersonal relationship tensions. Still others may need Biblical guidelines and practical advice on being a Christ-centered parent. Some may be seeking a more balanced life and how they can fit their hobbies and recreational interests into God's will for their lives. Others may be struggling with philosophical and theological questions about the presence of evil and suffering in this world.

Much of this information can be picked up by being a good listener. It can also be gleaned by a well-prepared, brief questionnaire. (See section on The Selection Of What To Study, page 77.)

Spiritual Maturity

When it comes to spiritual maturity, again, single adults are like married adults: they range from one extreme to the other. Let's take a look at where single adults fit into the range of spiritual maturity.

Many single adults are spiritually dead. They have never been born again. They have an inner restlessness and are searching for something to give completeness and meaning to life. They know little about the Bible. They often have distorted perceptions about Christ and the Christian life. They may even have some negative feelings toward the church because of previous bad experiences with contentious, self-righteous, or hypocritical "Christians."

Other single adults are "baby" Christians. They may have recently accepted Jesus as their Savior and are "on fire" for Him, eager to grow. Yet others have been Christians for years with very little spiritual growth occurring in their lives. They still are permeated with self, live by "sight" rather than faith, have a poor grasp on the truth of Scripture and are often very irregular in their meeting for corporate worship on Sunday.

There are also "adolescent" Christians among the single adults. They frequently read the Bible and pray. They regularly attend Sunday worship services. They regularly give a portion of their income to the Lord's work. They frequently have a place of service in the life of the church. Theirs is a growing relationship with Christ. Yet they have a lot of fears and insecurities about who they are, what others think about them, and what is God's will for their lives.

Then there are single adults who are "adult" Christians. They have a close, intimate, daily walk with the Lord. They have learned to hear His voice. They are quick to obey His leading. They have a deep level of freedom from the bondage of what others think. They have a genuine peace about God's presence and purpose at work through any negative circumstances in their lives. Their love for God and their trust in God are strong. They have internalized much of the truth of Scripture. Their lives give off the "sweet aroma" of Jesus. Yet they, too, have their inner struggles. They are increasingly sensitive to subtle aspects of self that have not been yielded to the transforming power of the Holy Spirit. They are more and more aware of how far short they fall of the perfection of God. They hunger and thirst to know Him more and to have the "rivers of living water" continually flowing through their lives for the blessing of others.

Additional factors to be considered:

Homogeneous or Heterogeneous Preference

Some single adults prefer to be in a class or study group with people in almost the same circumstance as themselves. If they are thirty-five, divorced, with a two-year-old and third-grader, they want to be with others who are of similar marital status, age, and have pre-teen children.

Other single adults prefer to be with those in different circumstances than themselves. For example, they may prefer to be with married adults who are older and who already have their children raised. It is as though they feel they can gain more help from those who have been "through it" and weathered life's storms than from those who are now basically in the same set of circumstances.

Those responsible in a local church for planning ministry to single adults would do well to provide both homogeneous and heterogeneous small group experiences for single adults.

Two Case Studies

Example of a Large Church

One large church with over 150 single adults was able to offer five classes on Sunday morning just for them. The classes were as follows:

College Class	made up of undergraduate and graduate students, never-married, ages 18 to 25 years of age.
Career Singles	made up of the never-married, divorced, and one widow, ages 18 to 30 years of age.
Adult Singles	made up of the never-married, divorced, and widowed, ages 30 to 55 years of age.
Make a Way Class	made up of never-married, widows, and one or two married couples, ages 55 years old and up.
Men's Class	made up of widowers and married men, ages 55 years old and up.

This same church was considering adding a sixth class for singles in the thirty to forty age range because there was such a diversity between them and those in their forties and fifties. Those above forty had children grown or almost grown while those in their thirties had preschoolers and grade-schoolers. Problems of space and teacher availability resulted in this class not being started.

Other single adults in this church chose to attend classes made up primarily of married couples. Often these were widows who had been attending that class before their husbands died. Some were divorced who continued to attend the same class after their divorces. Others tried a single adult class for a while only to decide that their needs were better met in a couples class. Usually, the factor that led them to make their decision was (1) having one or more friends in the class, (2) preferring the subject matter being taught, (3) preferring the teacher (personality and/or teaching style), and/or (4) not wanting to be isolated from married adults.

On Sunday evenings, the 30 to 55 age group offered a "Singles Sharing Session." This was a time of sharing needs, blessings, and spending time in prayer for one another. Although the session was open to all single adults, usually only members of that Sunday-morning class attended. Other singles went to one of the other adult classes which met at the same time.

On Wednesday evenings some singles ate together at the church supper preceding classes. Others ate with married friends. There was usually one class particularly geared toward the needs of singles. However, many singles went to one of the other classes because of one or more of the reasons previously mentioned.

Two of the Sunday-morning classes also had a home Bible study once a month. This afforded another time to get together. Many were feeling lonely and in need of frequent similar circumstances.

Example of a Small Church

This church in a college town had one class for single adults. It was for college and career singles who were in the 18 to 25 age range and had never married. Average attendance was about 12 people.

For a while the class also sponsored a weekly home Bible study. However, as class members graduated and moved away or got married, the weekly Bible study was dropped. Then, as some class members got to be 25 and older they did not feel they fit with the incoming 18-

year-old singles. They felt there was not enough of them to start a new group. They began teaching in children's classes during Sunday school or they started attending another adult class. A few even quit Sunday school all together. Attendance on some Sundays dropped to as few as two. Apathy had set in. The ministry of this class could have been revived and built up. A new class could have been formed for those "older" singles. There were other 18-to 25-year-old single adults in the area who could have been reached. But no one gave it the priority necessary for that to happen.

However, a new class for adult singles in the 35 to 55 range was begun. This came as a result of the request and initiative taken by two adult singles in that age range. One was willing to teach the class and both were willing to recruit single adults for it. All who attended were divorced (except for one widow). The class grew to about a dozen in regular attendance and really was a meaningful ministry to them all. Then the teacher moved out of town, one or two got married, and two or three began attending a couples class. After meeting for about two years the class disbanded.

Homogenity in age and marital experience was a reality in both single adult classes in this small church. But that was not enough to keep them from dying or being near death. Two other vitally important factors were leadership and desire. These two factors gave continued life to the single adult classes in the large church. They would have done the same in the small church if they had continued to be present. It only takes one or two who are "on fire" to get others excited and involved.

Leadership

It is great if a spiritually mature single adult is available and willing to teach a class of single adults. However, a spiritually mature married adult can do an effective job also. The important thing is that the leader know and love the single adults with whom he or she is called to work. The leader needs to be a good listener, one who empathizes with the problems unique to single adults, and who asks relevant questions to help them solve their own problems from a Biblical perspective (e.g. "What would Jesus do in such a situation?", "What Bible passages are relevant to this matter?").

In the large church example given, all teachers of single adult classes were married. All were effective in relating to single adults and in helping them relate the truth of Scripture to their unique needs.

In the small church example, the teacher was a divorced single adult who was effective in helping other single adults apply the truth of Scripture to their particular needs. He encouraged discussion and the people grew in their walk with the Lord as they grappled with Scripture in the light of problems they faced.

When the teacher in the small church moved away, he was replaced by a spiritually mature widow who had regularly been attending the class. Her input had been most helpful as a class member. But as a teacher, she did almost all the talking. When she did ask questions she paused only for one or two seconds and then answered her own question. People couldn't respond that fast and they felt frustrated. They began attending other classes.

Desire

The nucleus that forms a single adult Sunday-school class or home Bible study must have a deep desire for it to succeed. That desire must translate itself into regular attendance, contacting other potential members, and entering into class or group discussions.

The more who desire the class or group to succeed, the more effective it will be. When only one or two are really committed to make it go, it can go for a while. But if others don't catch the vision and enthusiasm for it, the vision and desire of the one or two will, in most cases, greatly diminish and/or die out.

In an informal written questionnaire sent to 100 Christian single adults known by this writer, only 14 returned their questionnaire. As surveys go, 14% is considered a pretty good response. Yet it is indicative of a real problem in working with single adults. The desire for being involved in an effective single adult ministry is

74

often not there. They may come for a while but if something more appealing comes up they often won't be found at Sunday school or home Bible study. This, of course, is not a problem unique with single adults. However, they are often more free to come and go without affecting other family members. Thus, on the spur of the moment they may not show even if they said a few days earlier they'd be there. This is why it is so important to have a core group of leaders and helpers (preferably four or five) who deeply desire to be together and to be growing in the Lord.

Methodology and Format

Of the 14 who responded to the informal survey, there was consensus that lecture should be minimal and that discussion, prayer, and fellowship should be the primary activities of a single adult class. This follows one of the basic laws of learning: people learn by active participation in the learning process.

One suggested format was (1) prayer, (2) discussion, (3) prayer, and (4) fellowship. This would necessitate advance preparation by class members in the study of Scripture and the questions or topics to be discussed. If this does not happen with at least several in the group, the discussion will often be no more than a "pooling of ignorance." To solve this problem, the teacher must resort to at least some lecture before moving on to class discussion.

Another suggested format was 1) fellowship, (2) prayer, (3) discussion, and (4) prayer.

It is wise for a teacher to discuss methodology and format with the class or group members. If they have had a part in determining these matters, they will also feel a responsibility to help them work. It will be their class or group, not just the teacher's. It will be meeting their felt needs, not just the needs perceived by the teacher.

Time and Place

The normal time and place for Sunday school is on

Sunday morning in the church building. However, if there is a desire for a single adult class and there is no space in the church building, a nearby home or building can do.

If the distance between meeting place and church building results in not being able to make it for the start of the corporate worship celebration, other alternatives should be explored (e.g., starting and dismissing class earlier, meeting after the worship celebration).

Home Bible-study groups could meet any time during the week when all (or most) group members are available. For those who do not work during the day (older widows, second-shift workers), a late morning group might work well.

For those who regularly participate in the Sunday-morning corporate worship time, Sunday evening or Wednesday evening may be a good time to participate in a home Bible-study group.

Although it is usually best to set a regular meeting date and time for home Bible studies, there can be flexibility when necessary.

There can be a rotation regarding homes in which to meet (each group member taking a turn). However, it is usually best to hold the meetings at the same home and switch only if a group member takes the initiative to request that the group meet at his house. The meeting in homes provides an informal setting that is conducive to sharing.

Balanced Spiritual Diet

A well-rounded spiritual diet for single adults includes such items as (1) personal daily devotions, (2) interaction with other Christian single adults in Bible study, prayer, and fellowship, and (3) interaction with married adults, other age groups, and those with different interests (yet having a common interest in Christ and Scripture).

When planning a ministry to single adults, it is important that they be integrated into the total life of the congregation. This can be done by encouraging the use of their abilities and spiritual gifts (singing in the choir, teaching in Sunday-night youth groups, leading Communion meditations, etc.). It can also be done by purposely inviting them to share in home Bible studies made up primarily of couples.

One of the most meaningful home Bible studies in which this writer has ever participated contained one "never-married" single with five married couples. This 30-year-old lady really appreciated sharing once a month with these Christian couples. They also appreciated getting to know and love her. Many of her comments and insights deepened the desire of the couples to have greater singleness of purpose in their daily living for the Lord. When she moved to another town, the couples gave her an attractive Scripture plaque to remember them by and to encourage her in her continued walk with the Lord.

The Selection of What to Study

A first step in determining what single adults like to study is to have all potential participants fill out the following questionnaire:

Church-Related Study Experiences and

Preferences for Single Adults

Name _____

Background Information

(1) Your marital status
     ( ) Never-Married ( ) Widowed ( ) Divorced

(2) Your children, if any (state sex and age of each child—also marital status if above 18 years old)

_____

_____

_____

_____

(3) Do your children live with you? Yes _____ No _____

(4) Your age:

18-21 ( ) 22-25 ( ) 26-32 ( ) 33-40 ( )

41-50 ( ) 51-60 ( ) 61-70 ( ) 71 and up ( )

Previous Church-Related Study Experience

(1) Have you ever been part of a Christian home Bible-study group? Yes _____ No _____

(a) If yes, what (if any) study was particularly helpful to you?

_____

_____

_____

_____

_____

_____

(2) What previous courses of study at the church have been particularly helpful to you?

_____

_____

_____

_____

_____

_____

Present Church-Related Study Experience

(1) What topic(s) or portion(s) of Scripture are you presently studying?

_____

_____

_____

(2) How could your present study experience become more helpful to you?

_____

_____

_____

_____

Future Church-Related Study Experience

(1) What topics and/or portions of Scripture would you like to study in the future?

_____

_____

_____

_____

_____

(2) When, where, and with whom would you like to study the above topics (e.g., Sunday-morning Bible school, weekday home study group, single adults only, single adults and married adults together)?

_____

_____

_____

(3) What type format or approach do you prefer in a church-related group study experience (e.g., time for fellowship, prayer, lecture, discussion, etc.)?

_____

_____

_____

_____

(Attach another sheet containing any other relevant comments or observations you would like to make.)

The second step in the study selection process is to summarize the data received from the questionnaire. This can be done by the teacher or someone the group selects.

The third step involves evaluating the summary statement and making tentative recommendations regarding topics that should be included in a master study plan for those single adults. A "study committee" made up of the teacher and group leader(s), a representative from both the class and group, and the person who has general oversight over adult Christian education in that church (e.g. the minister, single adult minister, director of Christian education, Christian education committee chairman, etc.) should elect its own chairman with step four in mind.

The fourth step is for the chairman of the study committee to prepare a proposed master plan of study topics for one to three years. It should contain a statement of proposed learning objectives for each study as well as possible resource materials. It should also reflect proposed studies for both Sunday school and home groups. The resource materials can be found in catalogs of Christian education materials, browsing in Christian magazines, etc. Any Bible-based book, audio or video tape series is a possible resource.

It is usually not asking too much for class members to buy their own books. It gives them a good resource for their permanent home library. Buying it also enhances the probability of their really using the book. Such an approach also eases the strain on the church budget while enlarging the possible resources from which to choose. If a video cassette series is used, class members can help pay for the cost through their weekly offering.

The fifth step is for the class and group to make a decision on how much of the master plan they are ready to accept (or what adjustments they want to make). If they only want to decide a quarter at a time, that's okay. Just reviewing the proposed master plan will keep them sensitive to the importance of looking at their Christian education experience from a long range view. It will tend to help them have a less hodge-podge, hit-or-miss, full-of-gaps approach to their spiritual development.

An example of a three year master plan appears in the following pages. This has been devised based on past experience with various groups of single adults and the input from the fourteen who responded to the previously mentioned questionnaire. It would need to be adjusted to each group based on the unique makeup and most pressing needs of that group. However, every one of the topics suggested could be profitably used in single adult classes and study groups.

YEAR ONE

Fall Quarter (September-November)

Sunday School—Survey of the Bible

Learning Objectives:
(1) To increase knowledge of the basic components and highlights of the Bible.
(2) To increase understanding of how the various parts of Scripture fit into one coherent whole.
(3) To increase appreciation for the Bible.
(4) To develop the discipline of daily Bible reading and application to life.
Suggested resource book—*Training for Service: A Survey of the Bible,* by Orrin Root (Standard Publishing).

Home Bible-Study Group—How to Discern the Will of God in Any Situation

Learning Objectives:
(1) To increase awareness of the factors that are involved in discerning the will of God.
(2) To think through past experiences and present dilemmas regarding the discernment of God's will in real life situations.
Suggested resource book—*How to Know the Will of God,* by Knofel Staton (Standard Publishing).

Winter Quarter (December-February)

Sunday School—Survey of the Bible (Continued)

Home Bible-Study Group—Christian Parenting for Single Adults

Learning Objectives:
(1) To understand Biblical principles for parents.
(2) To apply Biblical principles to present problems in parenting.
(3) To share how past parenting problems have been resolved.
Suggested resource book—*Help! I'm a Parent,* by Bruce Narramore (Zondervan).

Spring Quarter (March-May)

Sunday School—Principles of Interpreting Scripture

Learning Objectives:
(1) To understand the basic principles for wise interpretation of Scripture.
(2) To apply the principles of interpretation to passages previously not understood.
Suggested resource book—*Basics of Bible Interpretation,* by Bob Smith (Word Books).

Home Bible-Study Group—Freedom From Financial Bondage

Learning Objectives:
(1) To understand the steps to wise use of the financial resources God provides.
(2) To understand the Christian response to times when funds are tight.
(3) To experience increased freedom from worry or conflict over finances.
Suggested resource book—*Your Finances in Changing*

Times, by Larry Buckett (Moody Press).

Summer Quarter (June-August)

Sunday School—The Grandeur of God

Learning Objectives:
(1) To understand more fully what the Bible teaches regarding the work of God.
(2) To grow in loving God with heart, soul, mind, and strength.
Suggested resource book—*Knowing God,* by J. I. Packer (Intervarsity Press).

Home Bible-Study Group—Learning to Worship

Learning Objectives:
(1) To understand more fully what it means to worship God.
(2) To experiment with various Biblical expressions of worship.
Suggested resource book—*A Celebration of Praise,* by Dick Eastman (Baker Book House).

YEAR TWO

Fall Quarter (September-November)

Sunday School—The Preeminence of Christ

Learning Objectives:
(1) To deepen understanding of who Christ is and what He has done.
(2) To increase one's love for Christ.
Suggested resource book—*The Lord of Glory,* by Benjamin Warfield (Zondervan).

Home Bible-Study Group—Experiencing the Reality of

Christ's Personal Presence

Learning Objectives:
(1) To understand the meaning of "Christ in you" (Colossians 1:27).
(2) To share the difficulties encountered and the victories experienced in attempting to be consciously aware of Christ's presence within.
Suggested resource book—*Practicing His Presence,* by Brothers Lawrence and Frank Laubach (Christian Books).

Winter Quarter (December-February)

Sunday School—The Ministry of the Holy Spirit

Learning Objectives:
(1) To understand the Biblical teaching about the ministry of the Holy Spirit.
(2) To become more open to the Holy Spirit's personal ministry today.
Suggested resource books—*Heaven Help Us (The Holy Spirit in Your Life),* by W. Carl Ketcherside (Standard Publishing); *The Holy Spirit in Today's World,* by David Hubback (Word Books).

Home Bible-Study Group—Discovering My Spiritual Gifts

Learning Objectives:
(1) To be able to define the various spiritual gifts mentioned in the New Testament.
(2) To become clearer as to what are one's spiritual gifts.
(3) To discover new ways of serving God through the use of one's spiritual gifts.
Suggested resource books—*Discovering My Gifts for Service,* by Knofel Staton (Standard Publishing); *Your Spiritual Gifts Can Help Your Church Grow,* by Peter Wagner (Regal Books).

Spring Quarter (March-May)

Sunday School — The Privilege, Promises, and Principles of Prayer

Learning Objectives:
(1) To gain a better understanding of the Biblical teaching on prayer.
(2) To overcome any hesitancy to pray aloud in front of others when appropriate to do so.
Suggested resource books—*Jesus Teaches on Prayer,* by Ray Stedman (Word Books); *With Christ in the School of Prayer,* by Andrew Murray (Whitaker House).

Home Bible-Study Group — Laboratory in Intercessory Prayer

Learning Objectives:
(1) To deepen the desire to be a prayer warrior on behalf of others.
(2) To develop a workable plan for being involved every day in intercessory prayer.
(3) To practice praying with others for others.
Suggested resource books—*Hour That Changes the World,* by Dick Eastman (Baker Book House); *The Ministry of Intercession,* by Andrew Murray (Whitaker House).

Summer Quarter (June-August)

Sunday School — Fulfillment of Old Testament Prophecies

Learning Objectives:
(1) To become aware of the different areas of Old Testament prophecy with examples of fulfillment in each area (e.g. national destruction, personal blessing, etc.).
(2) To become more familiar with the many Old Testament Messianic prophecies that were fulfilled in

Jesus Christ.
Suggested resource books—*Prophecy: Fact or Fiction,* by Josh McDowell (Campus Crusade); *What the Bible Says About the Promised Messiah,* by James Smith (College Press).

Home Bible-Study Group—Prophecies Regarding the End of Time

Learning Objectives:
(1) To better understand what the Bible says about end time events.
(2) To become aware of some of the major attempts to fit all of the facts into a coherent whole.
Suggested resource books—*The Millennium: Four Views,* edited by Robert Clouse (Intervarsity Press); *What the Bible Says About the End Time,* by Russell Boatman (College Press).

YEAR THREE

Fall Quarter (September-November)

Sunday School—The Book of Acts

Learning Objectives:
(1) To get a greater grasp on the nature of the early church.
(2) To discover strategies for enabling the present-day church to become more like the church as God intended it to be.
Suggested resource books—*The New Testament Church Then and Now,* by LeRoy Lawson (Standard Publishing); *The Acts Trilogy,* by Ray Stedman (Gospel Light).

Home Bible-Study Group—How to Share Your Faith Effectively

Learning Objectives:
(1) To identify the hang-ups people have in sharing their faith.
(2) To figure out ways to overcome each hang-up.
(3) To become more comfortable and natural in sharing one's faith with others.

Suggested resource books—*Friendship Evangelism,* by Arthur McPhee (Zondervan); *How to Give Away Your Faith,* by Paul Little (Intervarsity Press).

Winter Quarter (December-February)

Sunday School—The Book of Acts (Continued)

Home Bible-Study Group—Developing a Healthy Christian Self-Concept

Learning Objectives:
(1) To help one get in touch with his true feelings about himself.
(2) To equip one to respond in a positive, Christ-honoring way, as opposed to being negative and rejecting of himself.

Suggested resource book—*Do I Have to Be Me?* by Lloyd Ahlem (Gospel Light).

Spring Quarter (March-May)

Sunday School—The Christian Response in the Face of Adversity

Learning Objectives:
(1) To develop Scripture-based thought patterns and actions that enable a Christian to persevere through hard times.

88

(2) To better understand the apostle Paul's ability to cope with adversity.

Suggested resource books—*Where Is God When It Hurts?* by Philip Yancy (Zondervan); *How Can It Be All Right When Everything Is All Wrong?* by Lewis Smedes (Harper & Row).

Home Bible-Study Group—Resolving Strains in Interpersonal Relationships

Learning Objectives:
(1) To honestly face up to present strains in any interpersonal relationship.
(2) To learn Christ-honoring attitudes and actions in responding to strains in interpersonal relationships.
(3) To begin putting into practice what is being learned, evaluating it and making adjustments where needed.

Suggested resource books—*Forgive and Forget,* by Lewis Smedes (Harper & Row); *Caring Enough to Hear and Be Heard,* by David Augsburger (Regal Books).

Summer Quarter (June-August)

Sunday School—Learning to Live by Faith

Learning Objectives:
(1) To understand more fully that God can be trusted in every area of one's life.
(2) To become more familiar with both Biblical and contemporary examples of people who lived by faith.

Suggested resource books—*Hudson Taylor's Spiritual Secret,* by Howard Taylor (Moody Press); *What the Bible Says About Faith,* by C. C. Crawford (College Press); *Faith to Change the World,* by Lester Sumrall (Harrison House).

Home Bible-Study Group—Learning to Live by Love

Learning Objective:
(1) To understand more fully what it means to live out the quality of Christian love described in 1 Corinthians 13.
Suggested resource book—*Love Within Limits,* by Lewis Smedes (Eerdmans).

Some observations about the above curriculum suggestions:

(1) Though each study is self-contained, there is often a logical progression in the order of courses covered when following a master plan.

(2) There can be a re-examination and change of the master plan at any point where new needs and desires of the single adults surface.

(3) Often there is no published study material that is geared to accomplish the particular learning objectives desired. When this occurs, it is usually best to find closely-related material and then supplement it with the teacher's and/or staff members' original material that gets to the heart of the learning desired.

What Some Single Adults Say They Like to Study

Of the 14 single adults who responded to the previously mentioned questionnaire, most expressed the desire to study various books of the Bible. Such comments were made as, "I would like an in-depth study of the book of Revelation" ... "Minor Prophets, any or all" ... "Acts" ... "Any part of the New Testament" ... "Any part of the Bible" ... "Proverbs."

Most all expressed the desire to study topical matters that directly related to their lives as single adults. Some of their responses included, "What the Bible Has to Say About Divorce" ... "Preparing for Marriage—Finding and Choosing 'Mr. Right'" ... "Knowing the Difference Between Acting in Faith and Making a Stupid Decision" ... "Finding Truth in Today's Culture (Music, Paintings, Art Forms) and How Today's Beliefs Are Reflected in It."

Several mentioned particular Bible topics they would like to study. These included such matters as "Prayer and Faith—the Interaction of the Two" ... "Baptism of the Holy Spirit" ... "How to Know the Lord's Will (and How to Be Productive During the Interim When His Will on a Particular Matter Has Not Become Clear)" ... "How God Speaks to Us" ... "What the Church Is" ... "What Belief Is" ... "Priesthood of All Believers" ... "Prophecy."

In summary, single adults want to know God's Word and how it applies to their particular needs and circumstances. By taking the time to get to know single adults, by getting their input on the type of learning experiences they are seeking, by praying for God's leading, and by giving freely of oneself on their behalf, every church can develop a meaningful ministry to single adults.

What a joy to feed single adults regularly on the Word of life! Their taste and capacity for the meat of the Word will increase. Not only will their inner wholeness and personal needs be met, they will become an ever increasing source God uses for the building up of each local church.

CHAPTER FIVE

About This Chapter's Author

Linda M Cahill

Linda Cahill is Assistant Professor of Industrial Engineering for the University of Minnesota at Duluth. Before that she was a visiting faculty member at the University of Cincinnati in the Department of Mechanical and Industrial Engineering.

After earning her B. S. in Natural Science from Xavier University (Cincinnati), she completed a year of clinical training in Nuclear Medicine Technology. Following a four-year career in nuclear medicine, she entered the University of Cincinnati to obtain a Masters Degree in Industrial Engineering. The emphasis of her study was on Industrial Safety and Ergonomic Design. In 1983 she was accepted into the doctoral program to further her concentration in safety and ergonomics. She completed that program, and received her doctorate degree in 1987.

She has recently completed two years of work with NIOSH (the National Institute for Occupational Safety and Health). While there she performed health hazard evaluations in industry and participated in field and laboratory research concerning applied ergonomics and office automation.

Linda has been active in several professional groups including the Institute of Industrial Engineers, the Human Factors Society, the Society of Women Engineers, and the departmental Graduate Student Association (of which she was the founder and first president).

Linda has been a Christian for slightly more than three years. During that time she has served as a president of her single adult Sunday-school class, the dean of a singles retreat, and is the fourth-time hostess of the Annual Halloween Party and Extravaganza.

–5–

What to Do: Activities for Single Adults

by Linda M. Cahill

Singles' groups have been wrought with varying degrees of success in today's society. Instead of focusing on the causes for failure among such groups, let's examine the strongest reason for their success—fulfillment of singles' needs.

For the most part, single adults' needs vary little from those of their married peers. These common need areas include financial matters, health concerns, professional and educational development, spiritual growth, Christian fellowship and social interaction, service, and emotional well-being. These needs tend to manifest themselves in different ways in the single person than in the case of the married individual. This is a result of the underlying subject that distinguishes the two—the existence or non-existence of a life partner. Certainly having such a partner adds a dimension of responsibility unknown to singles. On the other hand, not to have a life partner deprives the single of the benefits and privileges that such an intimate and lasting relationship affords. Thus, loneliness, the need to interact with other singles, dating, and the necessity of meeting all of the aforementioned needs (financial, health, etc.) without the help and support of a partner are the challenges confronting the single adult.

In order for a Christian single adult ministry to be successful, it must recognize these needs among its members and deal with them effectively. Planned singles' activities of various types are a means of fulfilling many of these needs—the most successful activities being those that cut across several need areas. The purpose of this chapter is to suggest such activities as well as point out when and how they might prove beneficial. The following is a brief outline of its contents:

I. Social Events
   A. parties
   B. games
   C. getting together for the day or just an evening

II. Health
   A. physical fitness
   B. mental/emotional well-being

III. Spiritual Growth

IV. Service
   A. ongoing
   B. projects

V. Financial

VI. Educational and Professional Development

VII. Retreats

VIII. Singularly Important Points

I. Social Events

Social activities not only present the opportunity for Christian fellowship, but they also provide some of the best chances for involving non-Christian friends. And let's not forget that they're a great way to meet potential dates and new friends!

A. Parties

Everybody loves a party! Singles are always looking for an excuse to get together—and what better excuse than Halloween, Christmas, New Year's Eve (in July), an apartment warming, a farewell. Any occasion will do. All you really need are the three essential elements: food, friends, and fun. (Notice that food was mentioned first in this list. This was no accident! After many years of intense observation, I have come to the unshakable conclusion that Christians love to eat! This, by the way, is another thing that singles have in common with married folks.)

Some of the most memorable parties are those that revolve around a holiday theme. Most holidays are thought of as family times. So get your "family" of singles together and celebrate. Two such parties have evolved into traditions within our group—the "Christmas dinner and white elephant gift exchange," and the "annual cross-country Halloween party and extravaganza." These parties are especially great because the children of our single parents can also join in the fun.

So, just what exactly is the "white elephant gift exchange"? Well, it's a method of exchanging Christmas presents for which you may never be forgotten. (You may also never be forgiven!) Each guest brings a "surprise" gift to place under the tree. The group is asked to form a large circle (this exchange gets better as the crowd gets larger) and the host or hostess chooses one guest to begin. The selected guest may choose to unwrap any gift from under the tree. The second person may choose to unwrap a gift or can elect to take the already unwrapped gift from the first guest. Proceeding around the circle, the next individual can go to the tree for a new gift or may take any of the previously exposed presents. If this person takes the gift from the first guest, then the first guest may once again choose a new gift or take one from someone else. The only other rule to remember is that you can't take a gift back from someone who just took it from you. Sound like fun? It can become absolutely hysterical when you get 20 or 30 people involved and everyone is running around taking each others' gifts. What makes it even funnier is that most of the packages contain totally worthless junk—things that nobody would ever (or at least *should* ever) want—true "white elephants." Some of the more valuable items have included a pair of broken tire chains, burnt candles, a cracked steering wheel, stale jelly beans, and a one-year supply of dates (every single's dream, right? Wrong, it was last year's calendar). To sweeten the pot, a few guests do bring nice gifts. This improves the chances of swiping, and gets things hopping.

For years the "white elephant tradition" has been the centerpiece of our single adult group's Christmas dinner. The dinner itself has been catered, treated as a potluck, held at a party hall, or taken place at one of the finer restaurants in town. Regardless of where the dinner is held, the Christmas social always includes the "white elephant exchange," a time for devotions, and a few crazy games (we'll talk about games a little later).

The Halloween party has also become a proven tradition. The event comes complete with food (of course), costumes, decorations, prizes, and wacky games (more on this later). For us, this party has become a cross-country event—for the past four years it has been held about 25 miles from the church, out in the wilds of Kentucky. It is a great place for bonfires, apple-bobbing, and outdoor games. Giving prizes for costumes is always fun, especially when you don't exactly stick to the traditional—funniest, scariest, most original, etc. One girl arrived dressed as a flirtatious witch and left with the prize for the "person who most needed to clean up her act." The prize was, of course, a bar of soap.

Holding a New Year's Eve party can be great fun—especially if it's in July. Party hats, noise makers, confetti, food, and, of course, the traditional singing of "Auld Lang Syne" at the stroke of midnight usher in the "New Year." The clever diehard will even go so far as to simulate the dropping of the big apple at Times Square!

This type of party is an interesting way to start a new single adult group. It is also quite effective in giving a new beginning to a group that is in a slump.

More party ideas include: Hawaiian luaus, beach parties, international dinners, cook-outs, progressive dinners, stuff-your-own-potato party, or make-your-own-taco party, Trivial Pursuit™ tournaments, and let's not forget ladies' night—a dinner hosted by the men. The following is an article reviewing just such a dinner. The article was taken from a Sunday-school class newsletter:

That's-a Nice-a

by L. C. Esquire

Where do you go to enjoy excellent Italian cuisine ... to be showered with delicate rosebuds ... to be serenaded by magnificient musicians?

Antonio's you say, or perhaps Delmonico's?

Oh, no-no-no-no! There is only one place in town where you will find all of this—THE PASTA PARLOR, home of the world-famous *annual* Fellowship Women's Spaghetti Spectacular!

That's right, after morning worship in the church parlor on February 12, the Fellowship men surprised the women with their culinary talents as they prepared a marvelous meal. This dinner of pasta and garlic bread featured the sauce of the Renowned Chef Ralpho. Entertainment was provided by a well-known traveling musician—bravo, Brad!

Azar, keynote speaker for the event, presented thoughts about Christian love between men and women. He pointed out the great potential that exists for witnessing and the need to overcome fears associated with such friendship-type relationships.

Yes, the first *annual* (dare we hope for more in the future, guys?) Fellowship Women's Spaghetti Spectacular was quite a success! THANKS GUYS! THAT'S-A NICE-A!

B. Games

There are many books which have been published containing directions for games which fit various types of groups in any number of settings. However, I have found that it really just takes some posterboard, a few felt-tip markers, some balloons, and a little imagination to create your own crazy games. Let me give you some examples:

1. *The Great Potato Race.* This is a spin-off from your typical race-across-the-lawn-with-a-potato-on-top-of-your-foot. This version calls for splitting the crowd into two groups, choosing partners within a group, and picking a slip of paper out of a hat which tells each pair exactly how they will be carrying that potato—either cheek-to-cheek, back-to-back, or knee-to-knee. Drop the potato and you and your partner must begin again. The winning team is the one in which all sets of partners successfully cross the finish line with their potatoes.

2. *Who Am I and What's My Line?* This is similar to the old game called "20 Questions" and works quite well with any size group. Simply make up a number of slips of paper, each containing the name of a famous person and his or her occupation (this also works for television or movie characters and their fictitious roles). Begin the game by having one person draw a slip from the hat. The rest of the group members take turns asking questions about the person or the occupation. When it is your turn you may ask a question or make a guess. The first person to correctly identify the celebrity and occupation will be the next to draw a slip from the hat. Here are a few ideas: Lady Diana—Princess of England; Hawkeye Pierce—MASH surgeon; Mark Spitz—Olympic swimmer; Barney Fife—Deputy Sheriff of Mayberry.

3. *The Great Pun-kin Chase.* This game was created as an outdoor activity for a Halloween party but can be

modified to fit any situation. Small plastic pumpkins are hidden in various locations. Hide one pumpkin per group in each location so that each group participating can find one (pumpkins may be numbered so that each group takes only the pumpkin corresponding to their group number). Separate the crowd into groups of three to five and give each group a list of puns which, when solved, reveal the locations of the pumpkins. The puns should be identical but should be given in differing orders to each group. This helps to spread out the groups. The first group to find all of their pumpkins wins.

4. *Treasure Hunt.* In a treasure hunt the crowd is divided into groups and each group is given an initial clue or pun. Deciphering the first clue leads to the second, and so on, until the treasure is found. Groups should be led from clue to clue in varying orders, with each group eventually recovering clues from all of the same locations—clues must be numbered so that each group takes only the clues corresponding to their group number. This game does involve a great deal of forethought and orchestration—but it's always a hit.

5. *Phrase of Fortune.* This game is a spin-off from television's "Wheel of Fortune™." The object of the game is to guess the phrase which is represented on a piece of posterboard by a series of dashes—each dash standing for a letter in each word of the phrase. The group is divided in half. Teams take turns guessing consonants which they believe may appear in the phrase. As long as one team continues to make correct letter guesses, they retain their turn. If they guess incorrectly, the turn passes to the opposing team. As correct guesses are made, the letters are put into their appropriate places on the chart. As the words begin to build, a team may guess the phrase any time during their turn. An incorrect guess causes control to pass to the other team. This game works well for theme parties. For example, Halloween phrases may include: Phantom of the Opera, Count Dracula, Trick-or-Treat, and The Bride of Frank-

enstein. Bridal shower phrases may consist of: Get Me to the Church on Time, Something Old, Something New, Something Borrowed, Something Blue; You May Now Kiss the Bride; and The Bride of Frankenstein.

6. *Puzzle Poppers.* In this game two identical picture puzzles are cut into pieces. The pieces are placed into balloons which must be earned by the members of each of two teams. The teams are created by dividing your crowd in half. As balloons are earned and popped, each group begins to build its puzzle. The first group to solve the puzzle wins. Groups may earn balloons in any number of ways. One suggestion is to hop to a finish line with the balloon between the knees. For a more sedentary group, answering trivia questions may be more appropriate. The puzzle itself consists of a series of pictures and letters which, when pronounced together, produce a phrase. As an example, a Halloween puzzle might contain the following four pictures: 1) the Jack of Diamonds playing card; 2) a can or bottle of oil; 3) an ant; 4) a picture of an urn-type vase. Together the pictures produce: Jack-oil-ant-urn (jack-o'-lantern).

7. *Make-Your-Own-Sundae Contest.* This game is always great fun—especially for those of us who always enjoy playing in our food. One only needs the usual equipment and supplies: ice cream (soft-serve works the best), chocolate sauce, nuts, cherries, whipped cream, M & M's™, and any other tasty food you would like. Challenge your contestants to make the prettiest, funniest, ugliest, and most creative sundaes. Don't be surprised to get such masterpieces as a clown with zits or Mount Saint Helens' erupting!

8. *Oldies but Goodies.* Let's not forget all of the old standbys—charades, "Name That Tune™," word scrambles, trivia games, scavenger hunts—to name a few. And, as described above, remember that it only takes a little imagination to transform an old standby into something new.

102

C. Getting Together for the Day or Just an Evening

There are countless activities which can be planned as social gatherings. Some may be planned as all-day affairs, others as evening events. Some are such that single parents may bring their children, others are more appropriate for adults only. There is an endless range of costs involved—from those activities which are virtually free to those which are quite expensive. The key is to vary your calendar of events to meet the needs and budgets of all the singles involved in your group. It is also important to access the needs of potential group members—are you consistently excluding others by the types of activities you promote?

The following is a brief listing of suggestions for various types of social events.

1. *Concerts.* In addition to concerts by popular and spiritual groups, symphony orchestras provide wonderful opportunities for formal evenings. Many such orchestras also provide series of free concerts in local parks and bandshells. Most larger cities also support a civic orchestra which provides free entertainment. This is also the case if your local university has a music program.

2. *Plays.* Plays are another type of event which comes in all shapes and sizes. Formal gatherings may consist of an evening at the local playhouse or dinner theater. More informal are the plays put on by local colleges, high schools, and civic groups.

3. *Movies.* In addition to the first-run movies shown at the more expensive theaters, many cities now have repertoire cinemas. All of the films shown at such cinemas are by request only. As a result these films are often old classics, foreign masterpieces, or unusual pieces with an artistic appeal. Another growing trend is the refurbishing of old pipe-organ theaters. Such theaters run old silent movies with the accom-

paniment of the organ. Finally, in the age of video cassette players, it is relatively inexpensive to rent a movie of your choosing.

4. *Parks.* A day at the park can consist of an outing at the local zoo, an excursion to your favorite amusement park, or spending the day at a water park (the latest craze in water slides and wave pools).

5. *Road Rally.* This is a wonderful way to spend a chunk of your day and get to know people a little better. Split your group into teams of about four per car. Equip each team with a set of directions and clues which will take them on a crazy course through your city or rural area. This is like a scavenger hunt in that teams must bring back certain objects in order to prove that they have completed the entire course. Such things may include match packs from restaurants, a receipt from a certain gas station, and information pamphlets from local parks. You may also instruct teams ahead of time to bring certain items along. If members are told to bring along an "instant-developing" camera then they can be required to bring back a picture of some obscure local landmark. They may also be asked to bring along a new toy suitable for a boy or girl child within a specified age range. Along the course, this present may be exchanged for a required object or a next-destination clue. The toys may be saved and distributed at Christmas to the needy children of your church or local community. The winner of the road rally will be the first team to reach the finish line with all the required goodies.

II. Health

An individual's health is determined by physical fitness as well as mental/emotional well-being. Good health may be promoted in both areas by studying the underlying health-related issues and by planning activities which lead to improved health by participation.

A. Physical Fitness.

Our nation is becoming increasingly more health conscious, and single adults are no exception. This growing concern is evidenced by an increase in physical activity, a greater awareness and improved knowledge of health issues, and a change in dietary habits to a low-sodium, low-cholesterol, high-fiber diet. Understanding of such issues can be promoted by inviting local speakers (possibly medical personnel from within your own church or single adult organization), or by organizing a group to attend community-sponsored talks, films, and workshops.

Overall good physical fitness can be promoted by holding exercise classes taught by someone knowledgable in the principles of aerobic workout. The instructor should also be aware of the limitations imposed by age, injury, and illness. In addition there should be greater attention paid to diet. When planning parties and picnics, plan to serve healthier foods. When dining out, choose restaurants with nutritious menus.

Finally, promote physical activities which are both fun and healthy. Such activities cover a wide range of interests, skills, cost requirements, and time commitments. Try to vary the types of activities to meet the interests, budgets, and time schedules of your members. The following is a listing of such activities.

1) Organized Team Sports

softball	volleyball
soccer	touch football
basketball	wallyball

2) Individual and Small Group Sporting Activities

bowling	horseback riding
frisbee™ golf	water-skiing
ice skating	swimming
roller skating	golf
bicycling	putt-putt golf
nature walks	tennis
racquetball	

3) All-day and Overnighter Activities

snow-skiing	caving
camping	mountain climbing
backpacking	bicycle marathon
river rafting	canoeing

B. Mental/Emotional Well-Being

As is the case with physical fitness, mental and emotional well-being can also be promoted through education as well as activities. There are plenty of films, videotapes, speakers, and workshops which cover topics such as the causes of stress, learning to cope, and the use of relaxation techniques. Since most of these types of programs are of secular origin it is important to view them with some measure of caution. Churches are becoming increasingly more aware of such needs and have taken steps to meet them. Christian mental health professionals are asked to give such talks and workshops as well as lead Sunday-school classes, Bible studies, and retreats. There is also an increasing number of films and books available to cover such topics as depression, loneliness, grief, fear, anger, doubt, and self-esteem.

It is important that a church or single adult organization be aware of the resources available to its members—establishing contact with a Christian counseling service, keeping an updated library, and maintaining a list of available films and videotapes. It is also essential that such groups promote Bible studies which deal with such issues, as well as encourage the use of prayer-partners and small prayer groups. It is important, especially for single adults, to be able to develop the kind of close one-on-one relationship that a prayer-partnership allows.

III. Spiritual Growth

Spiritual growth is the most essential, and often the most neglected, of all needs. Sometimes this neglect is on the part of the leader while at other times there is simply a lack of commitment on the part of the group members. Nevertheless, efforts should be made to organize activities which will promote spiritual growth.

Bible studies can be planned which deal with topics particularly applicable to singles. There are many books available which can be used as companion texts for such studies. High levels of participation and commitment can be encouraged by the use of a rotating leader scheme. Singles' Sunday-school classes may be organized along the same lines.

Other suggestions include the use of prayer partners, the encouragement of outreach activities, and taking advantage of planned singles' programs such as those of the North American Christian Convention. One's spiritual growth is intimately entwined with one's mental/emotional well-being. It is often quite difficult, if not impossible, to separate the two. It is, therefore, true that most activities which help to improve one will also promote the other.

IV. Service

Ministering to others is a very important element of personal and spiritual growth. Servanthood is at the very heart of Christianity. In addition, service provides the opportunity to utilize skills, abilities, and spiritual gifts in an uplifting and rewarding manner.

A. Ongoing

The goal of any group should be to encourage each of its members to become involved in an ongoing ministry—one that best utilizes his or her talents, attributes and gifts. Many times the activities that a person enjoys performing are the things that he or she does best. If strong interests are not present, one may make use of aptitude tests and schemes for ascertaining one's spiritual gifts. This may help the individual determine the ministry in which he may best serve. Remember—there is nothing wrong with trying several before making such a decision. Examples of ongoing types of ministries include:

1. *Teaching.* This includes such things as leading Bible studies; teaching children, high school students, or college students in Sunday school, leading an adult Sunday-school class; working with non-Christians; and discipling new Christians.
2. *Music.* Music ministries involves such activities as singing in the church choir, performing as a solo vocalist for a church service, leading an adult or children's choral group, and playing an instrument.
3. *Child care.* Providing child care during Bible studies, church services, and other activities. Child care is also welcomed by sick parents and in time of family crises.
4. *Handicapped.* Work with handicapped individuals might include signing as an interpreter for the deaf; reading news material, etc. for the blind; and providing transportation for wheelchair-bound individuals.
5. *Elderly.* Helping elderly members of your church and community can involve anything from washing cars and raking leaves to offering a ride to the grocery store to simply providing companionship.

B. Projects

In addition to ongoing ministries, there are many types of service which require a one-time concentrated effort to accomplish. These service projects usually require the skills and efforts of an entire group. In addition to providing service to others and allowing group members to utilize personal skills, these projects are also an excellent opportunity for fellowship. Some examples follow.

1. Organize a work day at your church or local Christian camp or retreat center.
2. Collect and send needed clothing and medical supplies to local and foreign mission sites.
3. Organize and maintain a local food crisis cupboard.
4. Stock and distribute food baskets and toys to poorer members of your church and local community.

5. Plan an outing for local handicapped children or become involved in the Special Olympics.
6. Organize and/or participate in work trips to distant and foreign missions providing labor for repairs to living quarters, medical facilities, and church buildings.
7. Hold activities, such as banquets and shows, for the senior members of your church.

V. Financial

In the times of spiraling costs, inflation, and unemployment, financial matters are certainly on everyone's mind. Singles are no exception. There are definitely concerns with respect to how best to handle one's money. These concerns may be addressed by sponsoring speakers and workshops on topics such as the following:
1. Taxes and tax reform measures—how these affect the unmarried taxpayer.
2. Financial planning and budgeting.
3. Investment options.
4. The single homeowner.
5. Stewardship.

VI. Educational and Professional Development

We live in a society that is becoming increasingly more complex and sophisticated. Thus, it is not surprising that most of today's singles have earned at least one college degree and hold some type of professional position. Since higher education and careers are such integral parts of many singles' lives it is important to provide counseling and support in these areas. Networking has long been a channel of information exchange and professional support within the secular world. Networking should also be promoted within and among churches. Consulting with established Christian professionals may aid prospective college students in career choices as well as provide guidance to the young professional.

Financial and scholarship counseling information should be provided. Information should also be available concerning how this type of assistance might be available within your church or group. If at all possible, promote the hiring of members into fields of prospective future career choices. Promote the use of aptitude and spiritual gift tests. All of these things will help in making more informed career choices.

VII. Retreats

Retreat weekends can be marvelous times of renewed spiritual strength and commitment. They also provide time for fun and fellowship and the opportunity to meet new friends.

Retreats can be planned successfully for many situations—as a kickoff for a newly formed singles group or newly undertaken project; as a new beginning when your group is in a slump; or as a source of ongoing energy and motivation.

A retreat can be held at a camp or retreat center or may be organized around an activity or trip. Camping, backpacking, river-rafting, caving, and skiing are examples of such trips.

Regardless of the setting, a retreat should cut across as many need areas as possible by incorporating a variety of activities. A retreat should include social events, times for study and spiritual growth, sports and games, workshops and talks on topics of general interest, and an element of service. Individuals have a variety of needs and a retreat is one of the best opportunities for ministering to the whole person.

VIII. Singularly Important Points

In the organization of singles activities there are several extremely important points to keep in mind.

1. Don't segregate your singles! Every planned activity should not be a "single event." It's healthier to organize some activities to cut across the barriers of mar-

riage and age. Singles and married folks, young and old, have a great deal to offer one another. Segregating your singles cuts off these important sources of enrichment.

2. Try not to overlook talent and ability in your own group. It is often said that a person is an expert 50 miles from home. This is sad but, unfortunately, quite often true. It is the wise person who realizes that you don't have to solicit an outside source to present a talk or workshop, or lead a Bible study or Sunday-school class when there is someone within the group who is perfectly capable and willing to do the job.

3. During parties and retreats, when games are played which involve teams, it is a good idea to split good friends and couples (married or dating) onto separate teams. This prevents the only-talking-to-one-person syndrome and helps members of the group get to know one another. It is also easier for newcomers to fit in when couples and cliques are broken apart.

4. Make sure that handicapped individuals are not overlooked. Be sure that requisite transportation has been arranged and that activities are planned which can be enjoyed by all.

5. A host, hostess, organizer, or leader should always remember that, once an activity has been planned, and the wheels are in motion, he or she should just go with the flow. Be flexible and enjoy yourself— everyone else will too!

6. Finally, and perhaps most importantly, *do not* put the responsibility for organizing and/or leading all singles activities on the shoulders of one person! A successful singles program requires the help, cooperation, and support of all its members as well as the church or sponsoring institution.

CHAPTER SIX

About This Chapter's Author

Dennis Chamberle

See Page Six

—6—

Single Adult Ministry: A Personal Perspective

by Dennis Chamberlain

My introduction to single adult ministry occurred in 1976, although, at the time I had very little understanding about what was developing. Armed with a Bible college education (where a request for information about "singles" would have received polite directions to the cafeteria . . ."she can give you change there"), and an associate minister's job description ("minister of everything that comes your way"), I began to work on the problem of what to do with our small cluster of young, single people. They weren't youth anymore and they didn't fit in with the married groups. In the absence of immediate solutions or strategies, I did the one thing I had been well trained for—I called a committee together.

From this simple committee meeting, a leadership team emerged with goals and strategies for the beginning of a single adult ministry. Within the first year we had established a solid leadership group, some organizational structure, a regular Bible study, and an active social calendar. In the second year we had a dynamic music team, two regular meetings, (Sunday and Wednesday) and a core group of 20 to 25 people. By this time I was spending about 10 hours per week in developing this ministry.

The following year brought continued growth; we were operating a very active program which involved singles 20 to 45 years of age. We moved our Sunday-morning class to a nearby pizza restaurant, held weekly volleyball games at a local college campus, sponsored community-related seminars and activities, and became an important element in the makeup of our congregation. By this time we were seeing 45 to 50 people in attendance each week. My "staff time" investment was about 20 hours per week in this phase of growth. The ministry continued at this level until 1982, when I accepted a new position as singles minister at a large congregation in southern California.

At the present time I operate a single adult program which involves approximately 150 people in its various activities. Our Sunday-morning class attracts about 60 people each week and our weekday study groups involve about the same number. Numerous activities fill our calendar each month—recreational, educational, study groups, prayer circles, and special group projects. Congregational support for our single people is very strong and we enjoy a very positive reputation throughout our local community and county.

These background notes are offered to provide a context for the following comments concerning single adult work. Over the course of the past 10 years I have learned many important lessons from both small and large church settings. I have experienced some very gratifying successes as well as some very disappointing failures. This chapter presents a variety of personal observations and feelings—shared in a rather candid style—in the hope that those who choose singles ministry can learn what to expect (both good and bad), what to watch out for (there are some problems!), and, generally, how to make sense out of this exciting, frustrating, challenging, and rewarding ministry.

I would begin by saying that single adult ministry is complex and difficult ... and comparatively few ministers are either willing or capable of engaging in it successfully. There are several reasons for this. In the first place, singles work usually involves a great deal of 'emergency room' ministry. For the most part we deal with people between the ages of 25 and 50 years old—many of whom are struggling through some kind of

116

crisis or transition. These are people who are hurting because of loneliness, relationship break-ups, single parent burn-out, severe disillusionment concerning the "victorious Christian life," and serious anxiety problems related to their futures. It is not an easy thing for a minister to face every day. In addition to this, these hurting, struggling, often angry people are not interested in pat answers or simplistic formulas taken from a three-point sermon. They want someone to listen to them, to share their bitter bread with them, to give them love and guidance through an often crazy and disappointing world.

Complexity and ambiguity characterize much of this area of ministry. It seems that simple explanations for difficult problems work well for certain groups within the church (perhaps children, youth, and young-married people) but single adults tend to expect more. This is especially true for those who have experienced a divorce or death. Life is no longer a simple black and white proposition. And the minister who steps into the lives of single adults (especially those who are unchurched) and fails to understand this will be destined for disappointment.

There is also a positive side to this picture. I have found singles work to be very stimulating and rewarding because of these same factors! These people don't want to attend church just to pass the time—they have real needs, difficult questions, and many areas of doubt and resistance which they expect me (the single adult minister) to respond to. This is the kind of ministry that keeps one fresh and growing! In addition to this, many of today's singles are rejected by the church (particularly divorced singles) or, at least, regarded with suspicion. To serve these people reminds one that Jesus came to minister to the sick—not the well; and we carry on the work of the Lord Jesus when we reach out to the alienated, the disenfranchised, and the sinner.

So, for all practical purposes, assume that an effective single adult ministry is one that can reach this difficult sector of the single adult world. Aim for those individuals in the 25-to 50-years-of-age bracket (you simply cannot reach *everyone),* plan to encounter some very tough customers, give yourself to it completely, and expect God to help you with the rest.

Singles work tends to take on a somewhat non-traditional flavor—perhaps in the same way that missionary work might when compared to domestic ministry. In fact, the "mission mindset" is helpful in developing an effective ministry to singles. As a "missionary" to singles, I do all that I can to learn of their culture, language, habits, and world view. I then attempt to "translate" Christianity for them in a way that they can relate to and grab hold of. Because of this view I will sometimes describe our singles program as an "organizational halfway house" for singles. They can enter the Church of Jesus Christ through our doors, whereas in most cases they would remain outsiders due to mistrust and misunderstanding.

Occasionally, a church leader who has developed an interest in single adult ministry will say to me "we plan to begin working with singles—but we don't want them to be an isolated group. We plan to integrate them into our church from the beginning ... no separate class or separate identity--we want them to be a part of everything." Even when this approach is based upon good intentions, it doesn't work. More often than not, it seems to be an attempt to *appear* to be ministering to singles, while at the same time not upsetting the status quo.

In order to develop a successful outreach program for single adults, it is essential to treat them "separately" ... just as you would with youth. The strategy may seem odd to some, but it really makes good sense! I have learned that it works best to establish a unique identity niche for our singles and to treat them almost as a separate population. However, that isn't the end of it; as soon as some strength and stability have developed, we begin looking for ways to modify the system. We work on building bridges *back* to other groups within the congregation and thus a certain amount of integration takes place. Some examples of bridging: a volleyball game with the high school department; a bike ride to the beach with the young marrieds; a special dinner party at the church with the "senior saints" class. When these types of activities are done on a regular basis, the single adult sector becomes a very important and well-connected part of the church body.

At some point, once you've decided that a singles ministry is needed, you will likely be required to face the elders and explain yourself. Do not be surprised if your idea is treated with coolness or even resistance; on the other hand, don't let this response deter you. The vast majority of churches in America do not have any kind of formal singles work . . . and they never have. It is clearly a new kid in the church ministry neighborhood. Because of this you will likely encounter a cautious and tentative attitude among ministers and elders when you attempt to begin something. Church leaders take this standoffish posture partly because they are faced with the new and unknown, and partly because the terms "singles ministry" conjures up a mix of negative images. For example: the Sunday-school class turning into a dating center or "pick-up" market; or divorced people in gatherings that make it look like they are actually happy and are having a good time. For many church leaders these images are incongruent with the kind of atmosphere for which the church should strive.

This is a serious issue. It is very important that you have the genuine support of your senior minister and elders. If you don't, a healthy singles ministry cannot develop. It will either die early in its development or be sabotaged later on down the line. And, it doesn't help very much to simply criticize church leaders for their negative thinking on this point. I had some of the same concerns when I first began in singles work. My concerns stemmed, in part, from the fact that I was a married person, coming from a "married mindset" which tended to be conservative (socially) and somewhat parental or moralistic. In addition to this, our church had not done this before, and we weren't quite sure what would happen.

I see a different picture now. I realize now that socializing and "coupling up" is very natural; and our church functions are wonderful settings for this to occur. We smile when we observe it happening among our youth ... and we condone and support it as a basic social institution among our marrieds; however, it feels a bit awkward when grown-up men and women carry on like teenagers! I agree wholeheartedly—but then, we are living in awkward times. Never before in our history, or anyone else's, has there been anything like the current single adult phenomenon.

Today, in America, we have literally *millions* of mature singles (those beyond college years, with previous marriage experience, or with children) who in previous historical periods would have been married and settled down. But here they are—caught up in the dating and mating game, struggling to manage their sexuality, often frustrated or troubled over the absence of familiar structure in their lives (which for many seems to be a necessary prerequisite for further maturity and life-plan development), and, in general, wandering about in what feels like an extended period of adolescence. Is it any wonder that our churches puzzle over just what to do with these people? They don't easily fit into the traditional church setting; and, as a result, they have become, in certain respects, an "unchurched" part of today's adult population.

This is the current scenario. Because of these factors, singles ministry can be very complex and difficult—and certainly unique. The minister who ventures into this area should treat it somewhat like the inventor with the experimental automobile: proceed tentatively and open-mindedly, don't depend too much on old theories, plan to learn from trial and error, and expect some raised eyebrows from your colleagues.

As in any other field of endeavor, it is very important to develop some basic goals and aims. This is important not only for the sake of the developing program, but it also helps your church leadership (i.e. minister and elders) relax and become supportive of your efforts. Additionally, it will play an important part in the formation of an identity for your singles group. Once these concepts are hammered out, they should be developed into some type of document and distributed (and clearly presented) to your church leaders and your single people. The following ideas reflect the plan I have operated with over the years.

Organizationally, my "working plan" consists of several parts: an overall purpose statement; a description of my general aim; a list of goals; and a sub-listing of specific objectives beneath each goal. The "purpose statement" needs to express, in simple terms, the same ministry philosophy that the elders are using to direct the church with; for example:

"As a church, we exist to reach anyone we can with the gospel of Jesus Christ and bring them into the kingdom of God (evangelism); and then, to nurture them in the love and truth of God (discipleship)."

All ministries within a congregation should operate from a common premise. Next, our general aim in regard to single adults:

"To establish and develop a community of single adults within the larger community of our congregation."

Following this are the goals which speak of the distinct areas we desire to develop:
1. To facilitate the entrance of single people into our church body.
2. To help singles go beyond entrance level participation and become significantly integrated and connected.
3. To develop a social network and support system for singles (an alternative to secular offerings).
4. To develop an "outreach base" for the work of evangelism.
5. To provide resources and opportunities for personal growth and discipleship.

From this list of goals I will develop, with the help of several key people from the singles group, a number of objectives to go with each goal. The objectives spell out the concrete steps we will take in order to realize the goal. For example, under goal number one we might add:

A. Establish a regular Sunday-school class.
B. Put on a special seminar—in the church building—and advertise it in the community.
C. Begin regular volleyball games at a local park or college campus.

Under goal number two we would list something like:

A. Encourage singles to participate as Sunday-school teachers, ushers or greeters, and committee members.
B. Involve single adults in the Sunday-morning worship service.

Whatever objectives are developed, it is very important that your single people take a part in their formulation. It is also important that these be concrete and measurable, so that periodically you can evaluate the process.

Looking at all of these ideas together, it is not an exaggeration to say that the three most important elements involved in the creation and launching of a successful singles ministry are 1) supportive church leadership; 2) a leadership team made up of singles; and 3) an organizational framework and growth strategy to follow. This assumes that the person who takes on the role of "singles minister" will be someone who really cares about these people and their needs, problems, and dreams.

On a personal note, I am sometimes asked if I think a singles minister should be married or single. My answer to this question arises out of my own experience of being in both camps. As a married man, I was able to develop and conduct a successful singles work, and I don't remember ever feeling that my marital status was a hindrance to my ministry. On the other hand, as a single man now, I feel that doors for ministry have opened to me simply because "I am one of them." In the final analysis, I don't believe that a person's marital status is *the* determinative factor. What is more important is the leader's attitude, his rapport with the people, and his competence in leading. With single people it is especially true that a married person must "earn the right to be heard" before the single people will give their allegiance. However, being a single man and minister has its drawbacks as well. A single adult minister will continually be challenged by the dependency relationships that can develop with various women in the group. These women see him as somewhat of an ideal or model. Infatuations develop (on both sides) and tangled relationships are often the result. My own manner of coping with this is to establish a policy which states that I will not date the women in my ministry. This frees everyone up; the women can trust me—the men don't feel competitive, and I have some clear guidelines to live by. This is not always easy to do, and I have made mistakes, but it works best for all concerned.

Singles ... almost 70 million of them walking about in America today, most of them not involved in a church, many of them ignorant of the salvation offered in Jesus Christ. To reach these people and bring them into the kingdom of God, today's church leader must take bold steps. These people will not simply wander into our churches! With missionary minds our call is to go into the marketplace and help these people see and know Christ. To do otherwise is to compromise our faith and contradict our Lord's own example.

Resources for Single Adults, Ministers, and Single Adult Ministers

After the Flowers Have Gone, by Bea Decker (Zondervan).

Bachelor Fatherhood, by Michael McFadden (Walker and Co.).

Beyond Divorce, by Brenda Hunter (Tyndale).

Boys & Girls Book About Divorce, The, by Richard A. Gardner (Bantam Books).

But I Didn't Want a Divorce, by Andre Bustanoby (Zondervan).

Crazy Time—Surviving Divorce, by Abigail Trafford (Bantam Books).

Daddy Doesn't Live Here Anymore, by Rita Turow (Greatlakes Living Press).

Devotions for the Divorcing, by William E. Thompson (John Knox Press).

Divorce & Remarriage in the Church, by Stanley A. Ellisen (Zondervan).

Divorce and After, by Paul Bohannon (Doubleday).

Divorce and the Children, by Anne Claire and H. S. Vigevend (Regal).

Divorce and the Christian, by Richard Plakker (Tyndale).

Divorce and the Gospel of Grace, by Les Woodson (Word).

Divorce and Remarriage, by Guy Duty (Bethany Fellowship).

Divorced, by B. J. Smith with Irene Burke (Tyndale).

Facing Life Alone, by Marian Champagne (Bobbs Merrill).

First Person Singular, by Dr. Stephen Johnson (Lippincott).

For Singles Only, by Janet Fix (Revell).

Free to Be Single, by Elva McAllaster (Christian Herald Books).

Getting It Together: The Divorced Mother's Guide, by Lynn Forman (Berkley Medallion).

Growing Through Divorce, by Jim Smoke (Harvest House).

Half-Parent, The, by Brenda Maddox (New American Library).

Help Me Remember . . . Help Me Forget, by Marie Chapian (Bethany Fellowship).

How to Get It Together When Your Parents Are Coming Apart, by Richards & Willis (David McKay Co., Inc.).

I Didn't Plan to Be a Single Parent, by Bobbie Reed (Concordia).

It's O.K. to Be Single, by Gary Collins (Word).

Jason Loves Jane (But They Got a Divorce), by Jason Towner (Impact Books).

Marital Separation, by Robert S. Weiss (Basic Books).

Ministry to Single Adults, by Gene Van Note (Beacon Hill Press).

Momma: The Sourcebook For Single Mothers, by Hope & Young (Plume).

One Is More Than Un, by Debbie Salter (Beacon Hill).

Other Side of Divorce, The, by Helen Hosier (Hawthorne).

Our Family Got a Divorce, by Carolyn E. Phillips (Regal).

Parents Book About Divorce, The, by Richard A. Gardner (Doubleday).

Parents Without Partners, by Jim and Janet Egleson (E. P. Dutton).

Part of Me Is Missing, A, by Harold Ivan Smith (Harvest House).

Part-Time Father, by Rubin and Edith Atkin (Vanguard).

Pew for One, Please, A, by William Lyon (Seabury Press).

Picking Up the Pieces, by Patricia Chavez and Cliff Cartlund (Nelson).

Pulling the Pieces Together: Help for Single Parents, by Carter and Leavenworth (Judson Press).

Reach Out to Singles, by Raymond Brown (Westminster Press).

Remarriage "A Study of Marriage," by Jesse Bernard (Russell & Russell).

Remarriage, a Healing Gift From God, by Larry Richards (Word).

Right to Remarry, The, by Dwight Small (Revell).

Sex for Christians, by Lew Smedes (Eerdmans).
Single Experience, The, by Keith and Andrea Miller (Word).
Single Parent, The, by Virginia Watts (Revell).
Single, by Marilyn McGinnis (Revell).
Successfully Single, by Yvonne G. Baker (Accent Books).
Suddenly Single, by Jim Smoke (Revell).
Talking About Divorce: A Dialogue Between Parent And Child, by Earl A. Grollman (Beacon Press).
Warm Reflections, by Jason Towner (Broadman Press).
When Marriage Ends, by Russell J. Becker (Fortress Press).
Who Will Raise the Children? by James A. LeVine (Lippincott).
Why Christian Marriages Are Breaking Up, by G. Dahl (Nelson).
Widow, by Lynn Caine (Bantam Paperbacks).
Woman Alone, by Isabella Taves (Funk & Wagnalls).